HOW TO KEEP
YOUR CAR
MECHANIC
HONEST

HOW TO KEEP YOUR CAR MECHANIC HONEST

Vic and Barbara Goulter

Illustrations by Vic Goulter

Scarborough House/*Publishers*

Scarborough House/*Publishers*
Chelsea, MI 48118

FIRST PUBLISHED IN 1990

Designed by Debra J. Donadio

Library of Congress Cataloging-in-Publication Data

Goulter, Vic.
   How to keep your car mechanic honest.
   Includes index.
   1. Automobiles—Maintenance and repair.
2. Consumer education.   I. Goulter, Barbara.   II. Title.
TL152.G618   1990   629.287   86-42781
ISBN 0-8128-3110-1
ISBN 0-8128-6262-0 (pbk.)

To our Baker's Dozen—

Dana, Michael, Paul, Chester, Raymond, James, Melody, Daphne, Ross, Neil, La-Wren, Grahame, and Victor

—with love

CONTENTS

ILLUSTRATIONS

Introduction

This book is for anyone who has ever taken a car to a mechanic for a knock in the engine and come away hundreds of dollars poorer—with the knock still there.

You probably felt ripped off. And maybe you were. Mechanics exist who will take forty-five minutes to replace a twelve-dollar gizmo, and charge $550. There are even a few who will do nothing at all—and charge $899.

Anyone who held you up for that kind of money would be charged with grand larceny. But mechanics have been fleecing customers for so long that some apparently believe it's part of the job.

So, how can you know whether that huge bill you've just been handed is a fair charge or a fleecing? How can you even be sure the work's been done at all? And how do you avoid such agonizing doubts next week and next month and next year?

There are books and classes that teach you to do your own repairs. But what if you can't spare the time or were born with ten thumbs? There must be some quicker, easier way.

HOW TO KEEP YOUR CAR MECHANIC HONEST

How to Keep Your Mechanic Honest provides people in the United States and Canada with just such a way. Read it, and you will be taught (in the friendliest possible fashion) the basics about how your car works and what is most likely to go wrong. You will also learn how to convert this new knowledge into a simple method for estimating the costs of repairs. Armed with our FAIR PRICE FORMULA, you need never play Mechanic's Victim again.

How to Keep Your Car Mechanic Honest was written by an experienced mechanic in collaboration with a professional writer with no background in mechanics. For the writer to follow the mechanic's ideas, he had to make them as clear and simple as possible. Every effort was made to eliminate jargon and unnecessary detail. What *you* need to know was always foremost in our minds.

This book won't train you to be a car mechanic. But it will teach you how to deal with one—and how to keep him honest.

Vic and Barbara Goulter

HOW TO KEEP
YOUR CAR
MECHANIC
HONEST

1

Thinking of Your Car as Almost Human

THE FIRST THING TO REALIZE IS THAT YOUR CAR FUNCTIONS MUCH THE WAY YOU DO.

When you get to know it, you'll find it's practically human. (So is your mechanic, but we'll get to him later.)

Like you, your car needs fuel for energy. Like you, it must have air and water. Like you, it must be able to change directions, slow down, stop, and start up again. It must eliminate waste and protect itself against wear, tear, and stress.

In your own body, all this work is done by *a network of systems*, each consisting of several "organs" or body parts, each with its own job to perform, and with each system leading to the next and cooperating with all the others.

It's much the same with a car, except that a car is simpler. The components are called "parts" instead of "organs," but the process is basically similar. Just as the "thighbone's connected to the knee bone," each of a car's systems works harmoniously and cooperatively with the rest.

Now, let's look at what these systems do.

ONE SET OF SYSTEMS MAKES YOUR CAR MOVE:

The starter system converts electrical energy from the battery into the mechanical force that gets the engine started.

The fuel system pumps a constant supply of gasoline to the carburetor or fuel-injection system.

The carburetor or fuel-injection system, mixes fuel and air in the correct proportions to deliver to the engine.

The ignition system, simultaneously, delivers electric sparks to the combustion chamber, which is part of the engine.

The internal-combustion engine compresses the fuel-and-air mixture and exposes it to the sparks, creating a series of controlled "explosions" that drive the car.

The transmission system delivers the power created by the engine to the wheels, boosting or reducing it as needed.

The steering system determines the direction in which the wheels will go.

The breaking system slows and stops the car and locks it into place.

WHILE SOME SYSTEMS SERVE AND SUPPORT:

The generating system supplies electricity to the battery, where it is stored until needed by the electrical system or by the other systems that depend on electricity.

The electrical system runs the ignition system, the starter motor, and such auxiliaries as lights and signals, windshield wipers, radio and tape deck, and the cigarette lighter.

AND OTHERS KEEP THE REST HEALTHY:

The cooling system keeps the engine from overheating—and also keeps the passengers warm in cold weather.

The lubrication system pumps oil through the engine, reducing friction by coating the moving metal parts with oil.

The exhaust system gets rid of the burned fuel (waste products) left over from the process of combustion.

The suspension system provides cushioning between the wheels and the car body to reduce wear and smooth out the ride.

The air-conditioning system keeps passengers cool in hot weather.

WE WILL LOOK AT THESE SYSTEMS ONE AT A TIME, OBSERVING HOW THEY FUNCTION AND WHAT HAPPENS WHEN THEY BREAK DOWN, AND EXPLAINING WHAT IT TAKES TO FIX THEM.

We know that you're not interested in becoming a mechanic, only in learning how to deal with one. So we'll stick to the most basic facts and discuss only the most common and likely problems.

But first, we'll consider how to go about finding an honest, competent mechanic.

And how you can know—and get—a fair price.

2

Four Places to Get Your Work Done

WHAT IS A MECHANIC? WHERE DO YOU FIND ONE?

The answers to these questions are not as obvious as they seem.

FIRST, WHAT IS A MECHANIC?

In Canada, as in Europe, a car mechanic is a graduate of a training course and an apprenticeship program. He has taken exams and holds a certificate that indicates his level of expertise. In other words, practicing mechanics are expected to be licensed members of an organized, respected craft.

In the United States, anyone can call himself a mechanic. The National Institute for Automotive Service Excellence will give ASE "certification" to those who take and pass certain tests. But mechanics don't have to be certified, and many are not.

Not surprisingly, Americans have trouble finding *competent* mechanics. Anyone certified will have his certificate on display, so ask to see it. A certificate does not guarantee that a mechanic is honest or pleasant to deal with, but it does suggest that he will be at least minimally competent.

Aside from competence, there are many other traits that make up the *good* mechanic.

A Good Mechanic (Wherever You Find Him) *Will*:

- Discuss matters pleasantly
- Be informative
- Put estimates in writing
- Discuss the basis of his charges
- Show pride in his work
- Use modern equipment
- Have a neat and orderly workplace
- Be honest and competent

A Good Mechanic (Wherever You Find Him) *Will Not*:

- Demand your exclusive patronage
- Object to questions or second opinions
- Show contempt for your suggestions
- Refuse to give explanations
- Attempt to frighten or bully
- Make you feel like a fool

NOW, LET'S CONSIDER WHERE TO FIND A GOOD MECHANIC.

For most people, the first place to look would be some friendly neighborhood service station or a small, owner-operated garage. Actually, the sort of all-around mechanic who works in such places has become almost as obsolete as the good old family doctor who used to make house calls. For years, self-service gas stations, along with specialists and cut-rate chains, have been cutting into his territory. Now, with the advent of the high-tech car, electronics experts are grabbing a whole other share.

JUST AS YOU NO LONGER RELY ON JUST ONE KIND OF DOCTOR, YOU CAN NO LONGER RELY ON JUST ONE KIND OF MECHANIC.

There are four sources of service generally available today, which we discuss below. A fifth and very important source— **the dealership** is discussed in detail in **chapter 20.**

The Four Sources of Service Are:

1) Diagnostic centers for checkups and tests
2) Service by an all-around mechanic
3) Repairs at big service centers and chains
4) Work done by specialists

1) The Diagnostic Center

Automobile clubs (such as the AAA) have high-tech facilities for inspecting and testing your car. You get a computer printout or other complete report listing what's right and what's wrong—all for under $50.

These reports provide a kind of timetable for repairs. The report will tell you what can wait and what can't. You'll learn if you need front tires now, a tune-up soon, or rear tires in another few thousand miles.

If you're not a club member, consult your phone book Yellow Pages under *Automobile Repairing and Service* for an *independent* diagnostic center—one that does diagnostics only. A place that combines diagnosis with repairs has a vested interest in finding something to repair. If there are no independent clinics in your locality, then you'll have to use—with caution—a diagnostic center that also does repairs.

An annual checkup is as important for your car as it is for you. Diagnostics catch most problems before they become serious or dangerous. You can use the report to plan and budget ahead. It will help a lot to have it when dealing with other mechanics.

2) The All-Around Mechanic

Everyone dreams of finding a really honest, efficient, low-priced, all-around mechanic. Although a vanishing breed, some survivors still do exist.

This is a person who gets to know you and your car, a person whose judgment and integrity you can trust. The drawback lies in the advanced tests he can't make, the equipment he can't afford, the parts he can't stock, the specialized knowledge he doesn't possess. Because there are so many different car models on the road, each consisting of some 15,000 variable parts, and because new high-tech innovations appear every year, no one person—however honest or able—can hope to master such a complex field.

Of course, if someone knows *your* car very well, these drawbacks may not matter.

3) General-Purpose Automotive Service Chains

These come in three varieties:

The automotive service departments of big department store chains, such as Montgomery Ward or Sears, Roebuck. These service departments exist mainly to install and service their company's own brands of batteries, tires, and the like. They provide routine maintenance, not major work. Their service is impersonal but usually competent within very narrow limits. Super low-priced specials are common, but to take advantage of them, you have to know what you need and when you need it. (This book, of course, is going to teach you exactly that.)

The automotive chains, also called "parts and supplies" or "tire" stores. Like the department store service places, these regional outlets sell house brands at cut prices, but their selection of parts and service is usually larger. They are equipped to do most repairs, including major ones. They also have many cut-rate service specials. You usually wouldn't go to them for diagnostics—only for work you already know you need. You will have to discover which ones are available in your own area (they usually advertise conspicuously in newspapers). *Automotive chains are also the best source for information about the prices of parts.* You can phone them or go to their "parts counter" any time and ask the price of any part for any car.

Franchised chains that service cars of particular makers, such as Mr. Goodwrench Centers, which work on GM vehicles exclusively. There are also oil company franchises, such as 76 Protec, servicing most makes. These franchises do everything from maintenance to diagnostics and their mechanics are well equipped and trained. They are strongly recommended, although a bit costly for routine maintenance tasks.

4) Specialists

These come in two very different varieties:

One services a single basic system at cut-rate prices. Muffler specialists, like Midas Muffler, are prime examples. They concentrate on a few, very common repairs and do a high-volume, low-overhead business. Such places tend to do whole system replacements rather tinker-and-fix-it work. It's best to go to them when a whole system needs overhauling and replacing, rather than when you want a relatively minor repair.

The second kind of specialist does elite jobs at high prices, servicing air conditioners, electronic devices such as fuel injectors, or other luxury options. They believe that people who pay premium prices for cars would feel cheated if they were not charged premium prices for service too.

CUT-RATE CHAINS AND FRANCHISES DO A LOT OF FLAT-RATE, "ONE-PRICE-FOR-ALL-MAKES" WORK.

For many jobs, there will be one flat fee for all domestic cars and another, slightly higher, for all foreign models.

The catch is that you must know what service you need. But read on, and that won't be a problem for long.

THE FOLLOWING SERVICES CAN BE HAD FROM SPECIALISTS AND/OR CHAINS AT HEAVILY DISCOUNTED PRICES:

- Lubrication, oil change, and filter (50% off)
- Front end alignment (50–75% off)
- Automatic transmission servicing (50% off)
- Front disc brakes relined (30% off)
- Rear drum brakes relined (50% off)
- Cooling system winterized or serviced (40% off)
- Minor tune-up (25 to 75% off)
- Replacement of muffler (50% off)
- Engine replaced or overhauled (25% off)

In Our Opinion, It's Foolish Not to Take Advantage of Some of These Discounted Services.

We have found that chains and franchises are usually no less "honest" than other service sources, and most of the jobs they feature are so basic that "just anyone" can handle them perfectly well.

To Locate Discount Services:

Look in the Yellow Pages (under Automobile Repairing and Service). Read the papers. Listen to radio and TV. Scan your junk mail. Phone the auto chains or the automotive sections of Sears or Ward and inquire about their specials. Also, keep your eye out for signs in local garages and service stations.

Some All-Around Mechanics Try to Beat Chains at Their Own Game:

They take on a specialty, such as tune-ups, and advertise

them locally for very low prices. Or they post low flat fees for many basic jobs. Their purpose, of course, is to attract new, regular clients. Give them a try. You just might discover your automotive Prince Charming.

TO SUM UP:

UNLESS YOUR CAR IS STILL UNDER WARRANTY, YOU WILL USUALLY CHOOSE AMONG FOUR DIFFERENT KINDS OF AUTO SERVICE:

1) **DIAGNOSTIC CLINICS,** WHICH RUN YOUR CAR THROUGH TESTS AND GIVE YOU A PRINTOUT OF ITS CONDITION AND/OR A TIMETABLE FOR NECESSARY REPAIRS.

2) **ALL-AROUND MECHANICS,** WORKING OUT OF SERVICE STATIONS AND INDEPENDENT GARAGES, WHO TRY TO DO EVERY KIND OF REPAIR ON EVERY KIND OF CAR.

3) **BIG CHAINS** THAT SERVICE WHAT THEY SELL AND DO BASIC JOBS AT BELOW-AVERAGE PRICES.

4) **SPECIALISTS,** WHO DO ONE THING ONLY, BASIC THINGS AT VERY LOW PRICES, OR UNUSUAL ONES AT VERY HIGH PRICES.

AS YOU GO THROUGH THIS BOOK, YOU WILL LEARN HOW TO MAKE THE BEST USE OF ALL FOUR—PLUS DEALER-SHIPS, WHICH WE'LL GET TO LATER.

BUT FIRST, YOU'LL LEARN HOW REPAIRS ARE PRICED, AND HOW TO GET TO KNOW WHICH REPAIRS YOU'RE GOING TO NEED.

(DON'T WORRY—WE'LL TAKE IT ALL ONE STEP AT A TIME.)

3

The Fair Price Formula and Ten Steps to Honest Service

OUR GOAL IN THIS BOOK IS TO SHOW YOU HOW TO KEEP YOUR REPAIR COSTS TO A MINIMUM AND NOT BE GROSSLY OVERCHARGED.

Doctors overcharge. Lawyers overcharge. Suppliers to the Pentagon overcharge. Mechanics are no different. But they will be more cautious if they see you are aware of the factors that determine a fair price.

THE TWO FACTORS THAT DETERMINE THE FAIR PRICE OF AUTO REPAIRS ARE LABOR AND PARTS.

You probably knew that already, since you've seen these

costs itemized on every bill handed you by a mechanic. You also know pretty much what they mean.

What you don't know is *how much they should cost.*

FORTUNATELY, THERE'S A SIMPLE *FAIR PRICE FORMULA* FOR ESTIMATING THE COSTS OF LABOR AND PARTS.

Simple as it is, you won't always have to use this formula. Wherever practical, we will be providing up-to-date guidelines for acceptable rates for many common repairs. But since the cost of many jobs differs significantly from make to make, model to model, place to place, and year to year, you may come to wonder how you ever lived without the FAIR PRICE FORMULA.

To Find Labor Costs:

You simply multiply the per-hour rate by the number of hours a job takes. If you are charged $35 an hour for a three-hour job, then you owe $35 x 3, or $105.

Nothing mysterious about that. A baby-sitter, a plumber, or a psychiatrist all get paid the same way.

However, labor charges do vary from locality to locality. Different regions have their own "going rates." Wherever you live, you have to find out your local going rate.

The average "going rate" in the United States is $35 to $40 an hour. In general, it's higher on the coasts than inland, higher in urban areas than rural, higher in the north than in the south.

This means (as of this writing) that if you live in the exurbs of Hot Springs, Arkansas, you should pay well under $30 an hour, while New Yorkers or San Franciscans are being gouged for $45 to $60. (Canadian prices have their own separate structure.)

Go on, Arkansas. Gloat.

Find Your Local Going Rate

Talk to your friends. Ask your automobile club or your car insurance representative.

Phone mechanics and other service sources listed in the Yellow Pages. Say you are new in town and looking for a mechanic. You don't have to give your right name—or any name.

After three or four calls, you'll know what local hourly charges are. And you'll also have taken your first giant step toward getting past any phobia you may have about talking to mechanics.

All you are doing is comparison shopping. You wouldn't buy shoes or get a watch fixed without first asking the price.

How Can You Find Out How Long a Job Should Take?

This book will help. Any time we describe a particular part or system, we'll give you guidelines.

There are also other sources. Probably every mechanic in the land keeps a copy of the "mechanic's bible," the *Chilton Labor Guide and Parts Manual*. This annual publication suggests labor time for every sort of repair on virtually every car, as well as giving the price of parts. Many libraries stock it in the reference section and some book stores sell it. (Similar information can also be found in *Mitchell's Parts/Labor Estimate Guide*.)

If you receive a time estimate that seems excessive, ask your mechanic—or librarian—to show you the figures in *Chilton*.

Actually, *Chilton* labor figures tend to be overgenerous to mechanics. Guidelines put out by manufacturers for use on their own cars are more stringent. Still, you will not accomplish much by arguing with *Chilton*. Instead, use it as a standard of maximums. Don't let anyone ask for more time than *Chilton* allows.

Now we will consider the pricing of parts.

THE PRICE OF PARTS EQUALS RETAIL COST PLUS MARKUP.

If the retail price for a fuel pump for your car is $60 and there is a one-third (33.3%) markup, then the cost to you should be $60 plus $19.98 (33.3% of $60), or $79.98. You owe $79.98 for parts.

To learn the retail cost of parts, phone a big auto supply chain like Autotorium, Grand/Auto, or Strauss. These outlets have employees who do nothing but quote prices all day long.

We will give you some guidelines as well, but please keep in mind that there are some 15,000 parts to a car, and they vary in cost from model to model.

About markups: They may seem unfair, but they are a fact of life.

Your all-purpose mechanic cannot possibly stock all the parts he may need, and he can't buy in big enough volume to get discounts. He often spends time on the phone locating needed parts, then has to buy them at retail, and may even have to pick them up. The markup is what pays for this time and effort. In general, markups of one-third are reasonable and those above one-half are excessive.

Elite specialists often mark up 60% to 100% or more. They can get away with this because they have a monopoly for their services.

Cut-rate sources usually have what they need on hand and have bought it at discount, passing the savings on to you.

Some cut-rate sources provide parts at little or no markup, while others charge substantial markups for no good reason. When you get an estimate from such a source, find out their markup policy. You can check by comparing the price of the part on your estimate at the retail counter inside the store.

IN CHAPTER 5, WE WILL LOOK AT THE ARITHMETIC OF THE *FAIR PRICE FORMULA.* FOR NOW, LET'S CONSIDER HOW YOU WILL USE THE INFORMATION.

When you ask for any estimate, specify that you want the parts itemized and labor broken down into rate and hours. Then compare the charge for parts to their retail prices.

Compare the hourly rate to the local going rate and the time estimate against *Chilton*. If anything seems seriously out of line, get it clarified. If you can't reach a satisfactory understanding, go somewhere else.

Although some mechanics charge a deductable $10 for an estimate, it is still better to forfeit $10 than to overpay by $50 or $500.

If a Service Outlet Charges a Flat Rate for Services:

You can still check it out. Have the mechanic show you their list of flat rates, which will give a specific figure for the job to be done on your own make and model. Ask how long the job should take, then make up your own estimate, using THE FAIR PRICE FORMULA. If the results are within the same range, consider the flat rate a fair one. If the flat rate is much higher, try another service source.

THE *TEN STEPS TO HONEST SERVICE*:

First: Use the guidelines in this book to estimate the probable job and its reasonable costs.

Second: Use the phone to get more exact figures, comparison shop, and set up appointments.

Third: Be specific. Describe your make and model as accurately as you can. Do the same for the symptoms of malfunction. (We'll teach you how.) As you grow more confident, use names for specific parts.

Fourth: Get a written estimate of how long the job will take and how much the parts will cost. Have the mechanic say whether parts will be new or rebuilt, and tell him to use rebuilt if possible. Also get a written statement that nothing additional will be done without authorization from you.

Fifth: Ask for explanations if the estimate seems way out of line with our guidelines or the FAIR PRICE FORMULA. Maybe there's a good reason. In some models, certain parts are exceptionally expensive or inaccessible.

Sixth: Realize there may be special diagnostic tests and other expenses, especially during emergencies. Even so, if you come armed with the knowledge in this book, mechanics will be less tempted to take advantage.

Seventh: Instruct the mechanic to save all discarded parts for you to inspect and perhaps keep. By stating your intention to inspect and keep old parts, you put him on notice that you will have them checked out by some knowledgeable person.

Eighth: Once the work is completed, have the mechanic show you the wear on all discarded parts.

Ninth: Have him show you every new installation possible, and make sure they really do look new. You also want to make sure the installed part resembles the old one.

Tenth: Test drive the car before accepting it. Take nothing for granted and don't leave unless and until you feel satisfied.

TO SUM UP:

THE PRICE OF AUTOMOTIVE REPAIRS IS BASED ON THE

COST OF THE LABOR PLUS THE PRICE OF THE PARTS, WHICH INCLUDES A MARKUP.

THE *FAIR PRICE FORMULA* WILL GIVE YOU A "BALLPARK" ESTIMATE OF WHAT ANY JOB SHOULD COST.

THEN COMPARE YOUR MECHANIC'S ESTIMATE TO YOUR OWN.

ARMED WITH THE *TEN STEPS TO HONEST SERVICE,* THE GUIDELINE FIGURES AND THE *FAIR PRICE FORMULA* WILL HELP YOU GET THE FAIREST DEALS POSSIBLE.

4

The Starter System

**IT'S TIME TO LOOK AT HOW YOUR CAR
ACTUALLY WORKS—STARTING WITH
THE STARTER SYSTEM.**

**THE STARTER SYSTEM CONVERTS
ELECTRICAL ENERGY FROM THE BATTERY
INTO THE MECHANICAL FORCE THAT
GETS THE ENGINE STARTED.**

Its two main parts are the **solenoid** and the **starter motor.**

The First Half of the Starting Process:

As you turn the key to start your car, you will notice a click
and a bit of a catch about half way along. At the same time, a
red light will appear on the dashboard.

THE STARTER SYSTEMS

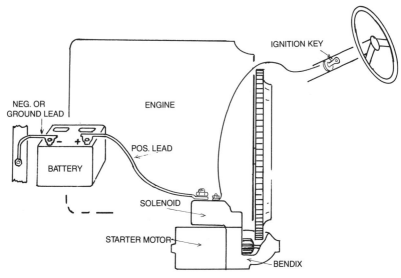

WITH SOLENOID ON TOP OF THE MOTOR

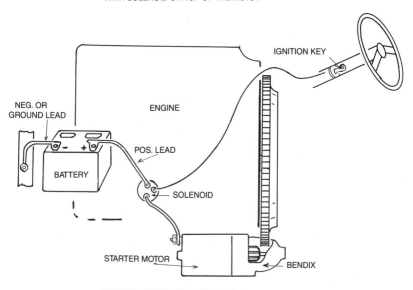

WITH SOLENOID BETWEEN BATTERY AND MOTOR

All this activity signals the activation of the **ignition switch,** which governs the flow of electricity from the battery into the ignition system—which we'll describe in a later chapter.

If you then turn the key all the way to the right, a second switch will go on.

This second switch is called the **solenoid,** and it governs the flow of electricity from the battery into the **starter motor.** When the solenoid goes on, it activates the starter motor.

That's all there is to the first half of the starting process.

The Second Half of the Starting Process:

The starter motor has an attachment called a **bendix gear.**

Once the starter motor goes on, the bendix gear grabs onto a part of the engine and turns the engine over and over until it gets going. Once the engine is going on its own, the starter motor shuts off.

And that's all there is to the second half of the starting process.

THE MOST COMMON THING TO GO WRONG WITH YOUR CAR IS FOR IT NOT TO START.

There are many possible causes for this, some having nothing to do with the starter system. We're now going to lead you through the process of locating a cause within the starter system.

Just follow along. If there are things that—in real life—you wouldn't be caught dead doing, don't worry. You're not expected to do them. We just want you to learn what is involved in the diagnostic process.

Diagnosis Is Always a Process of Elimination.

Let's say you turn the key and the car does not start. The process of elimination begins.

A terrible grinding noise would indicate problems with the **bendix gear**—which is very unusual. If there is no grinding noise, then the bendix gear is not the problem.

First test the battery by turning on the headlights. If the lights do not go on, or go on but are very dim, then you have battery problems. We'll deal with those in chapter 13, The Generating System.

But let's say that the lights do go on brightly. You'll know that your battery's almost surely not your problem. However, it takes more power to start your car than to run your headlights, and it may be that not enough power is getting through.

So you check the battery connections. You open the hood of your car and locate the battery. (See illustration.)

Connected to the battery, you will find the thick, red, insulated cable that connects the battery with the solenoid. This cable is attached to the battery by a kind of bolt called a "terminal." A black cable is connected to a second terminal.

You check the connections by trying to **wobble the cables.** If both are tight and secure, and there is not a lot of corrosion around the terminals, then you conclude that the connections are okay.

Now check the conditions of the cables, checking to see whether they look cracked or damaged. If so, they could be failing to transfer current to the starter motor. Damaged cables can be replaced in a few minutes and cost only a few dollars each.

(There is no danger in touching any of these parts with your dry hands, by the way, but don't let the acids get in your eyes or on your clothes.)

If the cables look sound, **consider whether your car is long overdue for a tune-up.** As we will explain elsewhere, this can contribute to starting problems.

But let's say the battery, terminals, and cables are fine and the car is in tune. The problem now has been narrowed down.

Let's Continue Our Process of Elimination.

We must now decide whether the problem is in the ignition system or the starter system. There are simple tests to determine this.

To test the ignition system, the mechanic could run a wire directly from the battery to the solenoid, bypassing the ignition. If the starter motor still did not go on, he would know for sure that the problem was not in the ignition system.

That would leave only the starter system. Because there was no loud noise, he knows the problem is not in the bendix gear. **That leaves only the solenoid and the starter motor.**

To find out which it is, the mechanic could now run the wire from the battery to the starter motor, bypassing the solenoid. If the starter motor goes on, he knows it's okay; the problem must be in the solenoid. If the starter motor does not go on, the problem must be there.

WHY DO YOU NEED TO KNOW ALL THIS?

Because, when you speak to a mechanic, you want to present yourself as a non-victim. You want to ask intelligent questions, understand the answers, make intelligent suggestions. If the mechanic gives you a song-and-dance about how time-consuming and expensive it is to diagnose starter-system problems, you'll know better. And you'll also be able to tell him that you know better.

If he starts playing games—telling you the problem is in the fuel tank, for example—then you can call his bluff. Because now you know which parts and systems are actually involved in the starting process. And if he says something about your not telling him his business, you will have the confidence to look for another mechanic.

Don't ever hesitate to question and don't ever hesitate to challenge. **After all, it's your car and your money.**

TO SUM UP:

WHEN YOU START YOUR CAR, ELECTRICITY FLOWS FROM THE BATTERY THROUGH THE SOLENOID TO THE STARTER MOTOR.

THE BENDIX GEAR (PART OF THE STARTER MOTOR) AT-

TACHES TO THE ENGINE AND TURNS IT OVER.

MOST PROBLEMS IN STARTING ARE DUE TO BATTERY AND IGNITION SYSTEM PROBLEMS, WHICH YOU WILL LEARN ABOUT LATER.

THE REST ARE DUE TO DEFECTS IN THE STARTER SYSTEM.

STARTER SYSTEM PROBLEMS ARE EASY TO DIAGNOSE.

5

Applying The *Fair Price Formula* to Starter-System Repairs

ALL THE FOLLOWING EXAMPLES WILL BE BASED ON CHARGES OF $40 PER HOUR LABOR AND A ONE-THIRD (33.3%) MARKUP FOR PARTS.

If you discover that the going rates are different in your locality, then adjust your figures accordingly.

THE SOLENOID:

In some car models, the solenoid is almost as accessible as the battery. In other models, it is less conveniently located on top

41

of the starter motor and under several other parts. These latter systems cost more to fix.

The most accessible solenoids take about half an hour to replace. The least accessible ones can take two hours or more. You can tell which kind you have by following the red cable from your battery to the solenoid and noting the location.

Solenoids themselves cost around $10. The average markup on each would be one-third of $10, or $3.33.

Let's See How the *Fair Price Formula* Would Apply:

```
LABOR ($40 x ½)   = $20.00
PART              =  10.00
MARKUP ($10 x ⅓)=   3.33
                  $33.33—FAIR PRICE FOR
                          A HALF HOUR JOB


LABOR ($40 x 2)   = $80.00
PART              =  10.00
MARKUP ($10 x ⅓)=   3.33
                  $93.33—FAIR PRICE FOR
                          A TWO HOUR JOB
```

As a rule, Ford Motors products have the most accessible and cheapest solenoids. General Motors, imports, and Chrysler Corporation cars are progressively more expensive in this regard.

THE STARTER MOTOR:

Starter motors cost $30 to $80, with GMs tending to be the costliest.

The job takes two to three hours.

```
LABOR ($40 x 2)   =  $80.00
PART              =   30.00
MARKUP ($30 x 1/3)=   10.00
                    $120.00 MINIMUM
```

```
LABOR ($40 x 3)   =  $120.00
PART              =    80.00
MARKUP ($80 x 1/3)=    26.64
                    $226.64 MAXIMUM
```

THE STARTER DRIVER (A PART OF THE STARTER MOTOR):

Very often, it is only necessary to replace the starter driver within the starter motor. If so, you will save one half to three quarters of your cost.

If your mechanic wants to put in a new starter motor, ask why changing the starter driver alone won't do. Let him convince you, with evidence, that some other part of the starter motor is at fault. Most mechanics, if challenged, will admit that fixing the driver would probably do. If yours does not, then seek a second opinion.

THE BENDIX GEAR:

Bendix gears cost about $20.

The job requires the removal of the starter motor and can take up to two hours.

LABOR ($40 x 2)   = $80.00
PART   =   20.00
MARKUP ($20 x $^1/_3$)=   6.66
                    $106.66—FAIR PRICE

Considering the constant pressures of inflation and other variables, prices within ten percent of the above figures are acceptable.

TO SUM UP:

ONCE YOU HAVE RESEARCHED YOUR FIGURES, THE *FAIR PRICE FORMULA* IS VERY SIMPLE TO APPLY.

USE IT TO CHECK OUT BOTH ESTIMATES AND FINAL BILLS.

6

The Fuel System

THE FUEL SYSTEM PUMPS A CONSTANT SUPPLY OF GASOLINE FROM THE GAS TANK TO THE CARBURETOR OR FUEL-INJECTION SYSTEM.

(For the time being, we will use the term *carburetor* for both carburetors and fuel-injection systems, since the two serve the same function.)

THE MAIN PARTS OF A FUEL SYSTEM ARE THE FILLER PIPE, THE TANK, THE PUMP, THE FUEL FILTER AND THE FUEL LINE.

When you fill up at the gas station, you put the fuel into the **filler pipe.** From there, it flows into the **tank,** where it is stored.

The pump, which is attached to the engine, draws fuel out of the tank and carries it through the **fuel line** to the carburetor.

THE FUEL SYSTEM

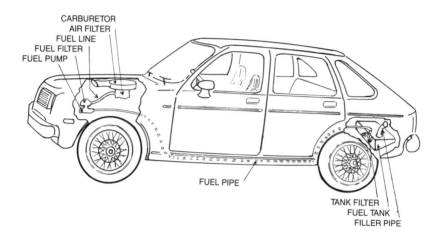

CARBURETOR
AIR FILTER
FUEL LINE
FUEL FILTER
FUEL PUMP

FUEL PIPE

TANK FILTER
FUEL TANK
FILLER PIPE

On the way, the fuel goes through the **fuel filter** to be cleaned.

This process is simplicity itself—except when something goes wrong.

LET'S LOOK AT SOME TYPICAL SYMPTOMS OF FUEL-SYSTEM MALFUNCTION:

Your car starts up normally, but then begins making a monotonous *hmmm-hmmm* sound and stalls; it does this repeatedly, perhaps every time you try to start . . .

Or it starts normally enough and manages to keep idling, but only in a bumpy, unsteady way . . .

Or it has been driving along perfectly well, but then starts coughing or lurching or even stumbling to a halt . . .

46

THE COMMON DENOMINATOR OF SUCH SYMPTOMS IS *FUEL BLOCKAGE,* WHICH CAN OCCUR EITHER IN *THE CARBURETOR* OR *THE FUEL SYSTEM.*

For now, we'll confine our attention to the fuel system, postponing the carburetor until the next chapter.

The first thing to suspect is that you're out of gas. It really could be that simple. Studies have shown that the single most common cause of fuel-flow problems is an empty tank. So check your gauge.

However, if you're not on empty, you may be using "bad gas." Some fuels on the market today are so trashy that they cause blockages known as **vapor lock** or **foam lock**. In general, these problems do not affect starting but come up during stressful driving.

To test for "bad gas," let your car rest and cool for an hour, then start it up. If it seems to run well, try it in very hot weather or under conditions when you have to idle a great deal in traffic. If your car starts bucking when it gets hot or is idling, your fuel may be of low quality. Try switching brands and going to the highest octane you can find.

(Even with quality fuel, **vapor lock** may occur under very heavy stress—such as long, steep climbs in extremely hot weather. Letting the car cool down for an hour—in the shade, if possible—is the best cure.)

THE MOST LIKELY CAUSE OF YOUR PROBLEM, HOWEVER, IS *DIRT*—THE GREAT ENEMY OF THE FUEL SYSTEM.

No matter how careful you are, some dirt can get in each time you put in gas. The gas itself carries its own contaminants.

The fuel filter is supposed to collect this dirt, but once the filter gets clogged it only adds to the problem.

Replacing your fuel filter on a regular schedule is the best protection you can give your car.

HOW CAN YOU TELL WHETHER THE DIRT IS IN THE FUEL SYSTEM OR THE CARBURETOR?

The mechanic—*not you!*—can disconnect the fuel line from the carburetor, then start the engine. If the fuel gushes freely and smoothly from the fuel line, then obviously the fuel system is not blocked. The problem must be in the carburetor. But if the gas fails to flow freely, the fuel system must be blocked.

Blockages within the fuel system are also easy to locate. The first thing to look at is the *fuel filter.* If that is clean, then a series of simple elimination tests can determine whether the dirt is in *the fuel line, the tank,* or *the fuel pump.* This process takes less than half an hour.

IF THE DIRT IS IN THE FUEL FILTER:

The cost of replacement—as always—will depend on where you live and what you drive. If you live inland, in the country, and drive a Ford product, replacing the filter might cost as little as $10, including both part and labor. It should not cost more than $25 for any car, anywhere.

IF THE DIRT IS IN THE TANK:

The tank must be removed, drained, cleaned, and put back. This job should take about two hours and requires no new parts. Your FAIR PRICE FORMULA should lead you to expect a charge of about $70, with adjustments for the local going rate of labor.

IF THE DIRT IS IN THE FUEL PUMP:

The pump must be removed and either cleaned or replaced. Cleaning takes about one hour and sometimes entails the replacement of a part, such as a valve.

(A valve only adds a dollar or two to your bill.)

Since pumps are readily accessible on almost all cars, the price of replacement varies little. There will usually be a flat fee of between $50 and $75, which includes both pump and labor.

IF THE FUEL LINE NEEDS TO BE CLEANED OUT:

The job usually takes between one and two hours. No parts are required.

THE FUEL SYSTEM IS SUBJECT TO ONLY A FEW OTHER PROBLEMS.

Fuel pumps wear out (as well as get dirty) and have to be replaced. A "pressure test" will determine whether a replacement is needed.

Tanks, pipes, or fuel lines can become damaged. Rocks in the road may penetrate them, causing holes. If the car is very old or the climate severe, these *parts may rust.*

Tanks, pipes, or fuel lines can usually be repaired, but must be replaced if the damage is too extensive. Because it saves labor, the replacement of moderately damaged pipes and fuel lines is commonplace. However, tanks can cost hundreds of dollars and are seldom replaced unless beyond repair.

Be sure to research parts' costs for your particular car, apply the FAIR PRICE FORMULA and always use the TEN STEPS TO HONEST SERVICE.

TO SUM UP:

THE FUEL SYSTEM CONSISTS OF THE FILLER PIPE, THE TANK, THE PUMP, THE FUEL FILTER, AND THE FUEL LINE.

ITS PURPOSE IS TO DELIVER CLEAN FUEL TO THE CARBURETOR OR FUEL INJECTION SYSTEM.

THE MOST LIKELY CAUSE FOR CONSISTENT MALFUNCTION OF THIS SYSTEM IS *DIRT*, WITH *BAD GAS* A CLOSE SECOND.

MOST JOBS WILL BE CLEANING JOBS, AND THE MOST COMMON JOB IS THE REPLACEMENT OF THE FUEL FILTER—AT $10–$25.

7

The Carburetor (or Fuel-Injection) System

THE CARBURETOR—OR FUEL INJECTION SYSTEM—MIXES FUEL AND AIR IN CORRECT PROPORTIONS TO DELIVER TO THE ENGINE.

Since most cars on the road still use carburetors, we will begin with them. Carburetors are more complex than the systems we have examined so far, but we will keep our explanations as clear and simple as possible.

THE CARBURETOR IS A SINGLE, SELF-CONTAINED UNIT THAT DOES FIVE INTERDEPENDENT JOBS, EACH HANDLED BY A DIFFERENT MINISYSTEM.

51

THE CARBURETOR SYSTEM

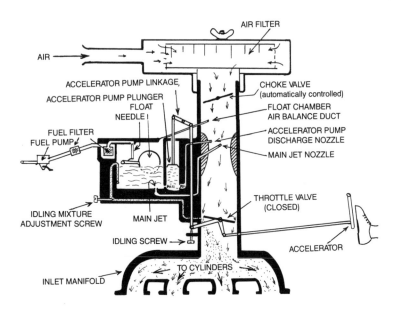

One Minisystem Supplies Air.

The air-intake system draws air in from the outside through tubes and a filter to the **choke,** where it is mixed with fuel.

Four Minisystems Regulate the Fuel.

1) **The float-and-needle system** allows only the amount of fuel needed by the engine to enter the carburetor.

2) **The idling system** provides enough fuel to keep the engine turning over while warming up, waiting at corners, or idling in traffic.

3) **The acceleration system** provides a burst of extra fuel when you increase speed.

4) **The main jet system** provides the steady flow that keeps the car running smoothly at higher speeds.

CARBURETOR PROBLEMS HAVE A CHARACTERISTIC PROFILE:

Hard starting, stalling, rough idling, racing, jerky acceleration, poor high speed performance, low gas mileage.

IT IS REASONABLY EASY TO PINPOINT WHICH MINISYSTEM IS IN TROUBLE.

If your car is troubled with cold starts, the choke (part of the air intake minisystem) may be adjusted "too lean"—that is, it may be feeding too much air into too little fuel. If the car starts right up but your gas mileage is poor, the adjustment may be "too rich."

Choke adjustments cost from $10 to $15, depending on your location.

If you get "flooding" without having pumped your accelerator, then you are getting too much fuel. The trouble's in the float-and-needle minisystem. (We'll go into the whole subject of "flooding" later in this chapter.)

If too little fuel is coming through, then the float-and-needle may be dirty or need resetting. The symptoms would be the same as if there were a blockage in the fuel system. As we mentioned in chapter 6, any able mechanic can determine which system is at fault by a simple process-of-elimination test.

If your car keeps stalling when you're idling the idling minisystem probably needs resetting. This is also true of *racing,* or

53

idling too fast. The idling minisystem will go out of adjustment in the normal course of use. Resetting is called an "adjustment" and should cost between $10 and $15.

If the car idles and accelerates well but bucks and jolts while driving at steady speeds, your mechanic should check out the main jet.

If it fails to accelerate normally, suspect the acceleration minisystem.

If it uses excessive fuel and there is smoke coming out of the tail pipe, then the fuel mixture may be too rich—possibly because the air filter is clogged. (There are, however, many other possible causes for high fuel consumption and smoky emissions.)

Before considering likely work on the carburetor system, let's clarify some of the terminology of automotive repairs.

WHAT IS MEANT BY SUCH TERMS AS NEW, RENEW, USED, MINOR OVERHAUL, MAJOR OVERHAUL, AND REBUILD?

New means exactly what you would expect: factory-fresh and unused.

To renew means to restore used parts by means of cleaning, grinding down, adjusting, and so forth so that they are "good as new."

Used means having had use without having been renewed;

used parts or systems may (or may not) be in good working order.

Minor overhauls (usually) consist of replacing all *obviously worn or defective parts* of a system with new and/or renewed parts. Such replacements are then fitted and adjusted to the housing of the system and to other parts that have not been replaced. *However,* different mechanics have different notions of "minor overhauls," so pin your mechanic down when he uses such terms.

Major overhauls consist of the removal of all working parts, the renewal of the housing by cleaning and/or grinding, and the replacement of the old working parts with brand-new ones. (A few working parts are customarily renewed rather than replaced.)

The whole system is then refitted, tested, and adjusted. *However,* some mechanics also have their own definition of "major overhaul," so pin your man down.

Rebuilding means renewing the housing and replacing the old working parts with new or renewed ones.

Rebuilding and major overhauling are virtually the same process. When done on your car in a service facility, the job may be called either "rebuilding" or "overhauling." When done in a factory, it is called "rebuilding" or "remanufacturing."

NOW LET'S APPLY THIS INFORMATION TO CARBURETOR REPAIRS:

Several carburetor problems often arise at the same time.

If one minisystem clogs up, others are likely to be dirty too.

Cleaning the whole carburetor is considered a "renewing" and takes about one hour. New parts, if any, should be few and slight in cost.

Several carburetor parts may wear out around the same time, calling for a **minor overhaul.** This takes about an hour's labor and costs $10 to $20 for parts (markup included). According to the FAIR PRICE FORMULA (and where you live), your total bill should be between $40 and $75.

Major overhauls, replacing all working parts, cost at least twice as much. Unless your car is quite old or has been given very heavy use, you probably won't need one. The job takes from two to four hours with prices ranging from around $100 to over $200, with Chrysler cars being the least costly and GMs and Fords the most. As with all major jobs, it's better to get estimates from more than one place.

Having a **rebuilt carburetor** installed can be cheaper than a major overhaul, because of the saving on labor. Research the costs for your make and model, then use the FAIR PRICE FORMULA to compare.

Do not let yourself be sold a **new carburetor.** It can come to $300 or more installed. Rebuilt carburetors are just as good and can be had for half the price.

MUCH CARBURETOR WEAR IS PREVENTABLE. AS WITH THE FUEL SYSTEM, *DIRT* IS THE CARBURETOR'S GREAT ENEMY.

Filters Are the Guardians of the System.

The fuel filter (previously discussed under the fuel system) cleans out dirt and grit before the fuel gets to the carburetor.

It is easily accessible and usually made of transparent material. Have it inspected frequently. One look tells whether it's clean or dirty. Installation of a new one takes only minutes. A new one should cost $10 to $25, installed, with Ford filters costing less than most others.

The **air-intake filter** (or **air filter**) cleans out dust and dirt from air brought in from the outside. In many cars it is located in a big, round container on top of the engine. (If not there, consult your owner's manual.) This filter is always accessible, should be checked on schedule, and can be taken out, cleaned, or changed in a few minutes. Filters cost somewhere between $10 and $25, depending on your make, and there should be no charge for installation.

DIESELING AND FLOODING:

"Dieseling" (also called "running-on") is unrelated to diesel engines, which we will come to shortly. It occurs when an engine continues to run on even after the ignition is switched off. What happens is that the air-and-fuel mix continues to flow into an overheated engine and to ignite spontaneously. *The overheating of the engine is the essential problem.* This may be caused by many factors, even something as simple as not enough coolant in the radiator. Occasionally, wrong—or wrongly set—spark plugs may be involved. Very often, however, there is some maladjustment in the carburetor, which lets in an improper mix of air-and-fuel.

Flooding the carburetor (often mistakenly called "flooding the engine") is caused when you pump too hard on the accelerator to get a cold engine started.

Perhaps the car is a little out of tune so it is hard to start. You imagine that not enough fuel is getting through, so you start

FUEL INJECTION SYSTEM

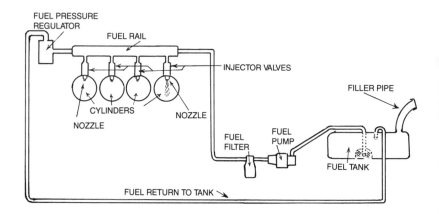

to pump. Actually, there is plenty of fuel coming through, so your pumping creates an excess. The result is "flooding."

A car with a flooded carburetor will not start, and the more you pump the more flooding you cause. The only solution is to turn the ignition off for about fifteen minutes and *let the engine stand.* This will allow the excess fuel to vaporize away.

When you start again, try it with your foot off the accelerator. If the car won't start that way, slowly push the accelerator to the floor and keep it there *without pumping* while again trying to start.

This approach will allow a lot of air to go through the carbure-tor choke and get rid of the excess fuel.

Expect a great cloud of black smoke from the exhaust when the engine finally does start. This does not indicate anything's wrong with your car. It's just excess fuel being expelled.

FUEL-INJECTION SYSTEMS:

Like carburetors, fuel-injection systems deliver fuel and air to the cylinders. *Fuel-injection systems, however, meter fuel to each cylinder directly.* This method is more efficient than carburetion and results in superior power and gas mileage.

Fuel injection is both simpler and more sophisticated than carburetion. Some systems are governed mechanically, but the vast majority use electronic sensor systems. No one standard design has been adopted. Different makers use somewhat different systems, which they are continually trying to improve. To work on them requires specialized knowledge, and able backyard mechanics, for whom carburetors hold no mysteries, dare not tamper with the electronic aspects of fuel injectors.

More and more new cars feature fuel injection rather than carburetion. This is in line with the progressive, competitive trends in the automotive industry.

FUEL-INJECTION PROBLEMS HAVE THE SAME SYMPTOMS PROFILE AS CARBURETION:

Hard starting, stalling, rough idling, racing, jerky acceleration, poor high speed performance, and low gas mileage.

Clogging of the Nozzles (or "Injector Valves" or "Injectors"):

This is a "bug" the size of a tropical cockroach, as many a proud owner of a $30,000+ car has learned to his sorrow.

Here again, DIRT is the great enemy.

Replacing fuel filters regularly and experimenting with grades and brands of fuel constitute the first line of defense against "clogging." Recent "high-detergent" fuels, available for fuel-injection cars, can be helpful.

When nozzles have to be cleaned, the job should take from one to two hours. No parts are required. As more and more cars come equipped with fuel injection, the premium prices paid for service should be coming down.

The Electronic Control Unit (ECU):

Engine sensors (called "the electronic control unit") send continual messages to the fuel-injection system, ordering up ever-changing supplies of air and fuel. If a "blip" develops in the unit, it will ask for the wrong supplies. It then may *seem* as if your fuel-injection system is defective, while in fact it's responding perfectly, but to defective instructions.

With any fuel-injection malfunction—unless caused by something as obvious as clogged nozzles or dirty filters—the electronic control unit should be tested as part of the diagnostic process of elimination. An ECU test should be a quick, simple process.

Your dealer (or brand-name specialist) has a virtual monopoly on the electronic aspects of your car, and you can expect him to charge accordingly. We'll say more about this in our chapter on high-tech and dealerships.

MAINTAINING *TURBOCHARGERS*:

Some higher-priced cars feature **turbochargers,** devices that force fuel into the engine by increasing the pressure upon the air-fuel mixture in the intake manifold. This results in greater power. Turbochargers require cautious handling. Abide by the manufacturer's instructions for any special care. Use the special synthetic oils developed for turbos and always cool the engine down (by idling for two or three minutes) before turning off the ignition. Otherwise, the high heat will cause damaging deposits.

Turbos also put pressure on the **intake manifold,** causing the gaskets to weaken. Replacing these takes about two hours. The price of gaskets differs according to make and cost more than they should since turbos are considered a luxury item. Check out the costs for your make and model, then apply the FAIR PRICE FORMULA.

DIESEL FUEL INJECTION:

Diesel cars use high-pressure injectors to spray fuel mixtures directly into the precombustion chambers of the engine. The high pressure in the combustion chamber creates enough heat to ignite the fuel without the need for a spark.

Fuel injection was invented for use in diesels, as part of the original design. Only later was it adapted to boost the power and efficiency of gasoline engines.

The advantages of the diesel car are its greater simplicity and power. It requires no ignition system, has fewer things that can go wrong, and so has the potential for being more durable, economical, and easy to maintain.

The disadvantages are that a diesel tends to be noisy, smelly, and a bit slow. It requires a special fuel that is not available at every gas station. To deal with heavier internal pressures, the engine sometimes has to be somewhat heavier reducing fuel efficiency. So the potential savings tend to be partly cancelled out.

In diesel fuel injection, the fuel circulates through **filters,** a **fuel pump,** and an **injector pump.** Work on either of the pumps takes around an hour. Filters should be cleaned and/or replaced on a regular basis—at least twice a year. Use your telephone and your FAIR PRICE FORMULA to ascertain prices on pumps and filters, which vary according to the make of car.

Because of the pressure on the **intake manifold** in diesels, the manifold will eventually need renewing. This is about a three-hour job.

TO SUM UP:

CARBURETORS AND FUEL INJECTORS MIX AIR AND FUEL AND DELIVER THEM TO THE INTERNAL COMBUSTION SYSTEM (THE ENGINE).

FAULTY CARBURETION CAUSES HARD STARTING, STALLING AFTER STARTING, IRREGULAR IDLING, RACING (PROLONGED, TOO FAST IDLING), "DIESELING," ROUGH RIDING, AND POOR FUEL ECONOMY.

DIRT IS THE GREAT ENEMY OF CARBURETORS AND FUEL INJECTORS, SO MAKE SURE THE AIR FILTER AND FUEL FILTER ARE KEPT CLEAN.

THE BRAND, GRADE, AND DETERGENCY LEVEL OF YOUR FUEL CAN ALSO AFFECT EFFICIENCY AND WEAR.

8

The Ignition System

THE IGNITION SYSTEM DELIVERS ELECTRIC SPARKS TO THE COMBUSTION CHAMBER.

For an explosion to take place, something must ignite the air and fuel. In gasoline engines, this is done with sparks produced by the ignition system.

IGNITION SYSTEMS COME IN TWO VARIETIES —ELECTRIC AND ELECTRONIC.

Since most cars still have electric systems, we will begin with them. Whichever type your car has, don't skip any parts of this chapter, but don't worry if you don't grasp every detail. Your goal is only to get comfortable enough with basic principles and terminology to communicate with your mechanic.

THE *ELECTRICAL IGNITION SYSTEM* WORKS IN FOUR STAGES:

1) **Production** of the current
2) **Timing** of the sparks
3) **Distribution** of the sparks
4) **Delivery** of the sparks to the fuel

1) Production of the Current:

Turning the **ignition key** starts current flowing from the **battery** through a **resistor** and **coils** to the **contact breaker points.**

This process "boosts" the battery's 12 volts to up to 15,000 volts or more, by rapidly creating and annihilating magnetic fields.

2) Timing the Sparks:

A **rotor cam,** driven by the engine, controls the "opening and closing" of the breaker points, while a **condenser** keeps the process going smoothly. This opening and closing ultimately creates sparks.

3) Distribution of the Sparks:

A **rotor** and **distributor cap** send the sparks through the **spark plug wires,** distributing them among the **spark plugs.**

4) Delivery of the Sparks:

The **spark plugs** then deliver these sparks into the **combustion chamber** of each engine cylinder.

HOW IT ALL WORKS:

Each time a "high-tension spark" is distributed to a spark plug, the "points" must first come together. This coming together allows the current to "flow," creating a magnetic field. Then the points "open" and part, causing the magnetic field to collapse. This alternation creates a "high-voltage current," which flows into the distributor cap, where it then goes to one spark plug after another in "firing order."

Amazingly, this series of events occurs *thousands of times per minute,* as long as the car is running. It happens so fast and frequently that the driver is aware of nothing but a smooth flow of power—*unless something goes wrong.*

REPAIRS TO THE IGNITION SYSTEM —*FLAT-FEE* JOBS:

These are simple adjustments or replacements taking only minutes. In the case of adjustments, you are charged the mechanic's minimum fee, based on some fraction of his hourly rate. In the case of replacements, you are billed for the part only, with no additional labor charge.

Engine misfiring is frequently due to a defect in the **distributor cap.** On most imports or Chrysler cars, expect to pay under $25 for a new cap, installed. Fords and GMs will cost somewhat more.

A **scope job** is a testing and adjustment of the whole ignition system, without replacing parts. It should cost $10 to $20 and should be done any time ignition system parts are reasonably new but performance is below par.

Spark plugs have to be clean, and the **gap** at each tip must be just the right size. Otherwise, the sparks won't get across as they should. Although some manufacturers boast that their spark plugs will last for years, don't believe it. Have plugs checked at least every 5,000 miles.

Cleaning and adjusting (or "gapping") spark plugs costs from $12 to $15 for most 4-cylinder cars, $25 or so for an eight, something between for a six. New plugs (if needed) cost under $1 each, so it's silly to try to make them last forever.

Poor spark plug *timing* can make your car "diesel" (run on) after the ignition is turned off, or cause it to lose power during acceleration. Adjustments take under 15 minutes and cost $10 to $15.

Although spark plugs are cheap and servicing them is routine, never underestimate their importance. *Poor spark plugs are the primary cause of poor performance.* Also make sure your car is fitted with the specific kind of spark plugs recommended by the car's manufacturer. You can ask at a parts store or dealership what sort that should be.

REPAIRS TO THE IGNITION SYSTEM —*FAIR PRICE FORMULA* JOBS:

These jobs are more complicated, requiring more time and/or more expensive parts.

Corroded or worn spark plug wires (or "high tension wires") occur in older cars. Cracked insulation or fraying produces the same poor level of performance as worn-out spark plugs. This sort of wear is clearly visible, and the mechanic should be able to point it out to you.

Replacing wires costs from $30 to upward of $90, depending on accessibility and the number of your cylinders. Expect the job to take 30 to 45 minutes on a 4-cylinder car; up to twice that long on an eight. Get the price of spark plug wires for your model (from a part sales store) and apply the FAIR PRICE FORMULA.

10,000-mile tune-ups (or simple "tune-ups") consist of replacing spark plugs and points, tending to the timing and condenser, adjusting the carburetor, inspecting and cleaning the battery, checking into the condition of the coils and switches, and other related tasks. Such tune-ups can cost anywhere from around $40 to over twice that much, depending on the size of the engine, the model of car, and local going rates. The job should take between one and two hours.

10,000-mile tune-ups are regularly available at much reduced one-price-for-all rates from chains and franchises. The tasks involved are routine and there is no reason not to take advantage of such savings.

Major tune-ups are more extensive. They include everything done for a 10,000-mile tune-up, with the addition of *a compression test* (for the engine), and *routine replacement of parts* such as the air and fuel filters, the PCV valve, the distributor cap, etc. This job, averaging between $100 and $125, can be a bargain for cars with busy or neglectful owners. Be sure to have the mechanic enumerate all the parts he replaces and supply their prices. He should also save the replaced parts for you to inspect and keep, if you wish. Total labor should not much exceed two hours.

ELECTRONIC IGNITION SYSTEMS:

Like electric ignition systems, electronic ignition supplies sparks to the engine. As with electric systems, these sparks must be produced, timed, distributed, and delivered. The main difference is in how they are produced and timed.

PRODUCING AND TIMING THE SPARKS IN ELECTRONIC SYSTEMS:

This process is much simpler than in electric systems. All that is required is a module of **transistors,** which are turned off and on by a **magnet** on a **distributor shaft.** Because this design entails so few moving parts and virtually no friction, there is nothing to wear out.

The system should be checked out annually with an electronic oscilloscope. It is unlikely that anything will need replacing. The module itself will need servicing after 30,000 to 40,000 miles. Your owner's manual will tell exactly when, and also when any wiring may need inspecting.

This simple but specialized servicing will probably have to be done at a dealership. *You will not be in a bargaining position.* On the other hand, these jobs need doing so seldom that the cost hardly matters. In fact, spark production in electronic ignition systems is a triumph of high-tech automotive innovation at its very best.

ELECTRONIC DISTRIBUTION AND DELIVERY OF SPARKS:

Unfortunately, this part of the system is not so advanced. As with an electric system, a distributor cap and spark plugs are

used and require similar servicing—with one major difference. In the electronic system, *the spark plug wires, distributor
cap, and rotor should not be cleaned but must be replaced as soon as
they show any wear.* The distributor cap will also need lubrication. Check with your owner's manual to find out how often
this ought to be done.

TO SUM UP:

BOTH ELECTRIC AND ELECTRONIC IGNITION SYSTEMS
PRODUCE, TIME, DISTRIBUTE, AND DELIVER SPARKS TO
THE ENGINE.

ELECTRIC IGNITION SYSTEMS DO THIS MECHANICALLY,
RESULTING IN WEAR AND TEAR THAT REQUIRE REGULAR
SERVICING.

ELECTRONIC SYSTEMS PRODUCE AND TIME SPARKS WITH
TRANSITORS, WHICH LAST ALMOST INDEFINITELY.

HOWEVER, BOTH SYSTEMS EMPLOY SPARK PLUGS, WHICH
MUST BE CLEANED AND "GAPPED" REGULARLY AND RE-
PLACED EVERY YEAR OR SO.

REGULAR TUNE-UPS, FOR ELECTRIC SYSTEMS, CAN BE
FOUND AT CUT-RATE PRICES AT SPECIALTY SHOPS.

9

The Engine (or Internal Combustion System)

THE INTERNAL COMBUSTION ENGINE COMPRESSES THE FUEL-AND-AIR MIXTURE AND EXPOSES IT TO THE SPARKS, CREATING A SERIES OF CONTROLLED "EXPLOSIONS" THAT DRIVE THE CAR.

HOW IT WORKS:

It is a basic law of nature that air expands when heated. And the more it is heated the more it expands. If compressed *before* being heated, it expands even faster and harder. In other words, it "explodes."

Explosions release energy, and energy can be directed to do

A SINGLE COMBUSTION CHAMBER

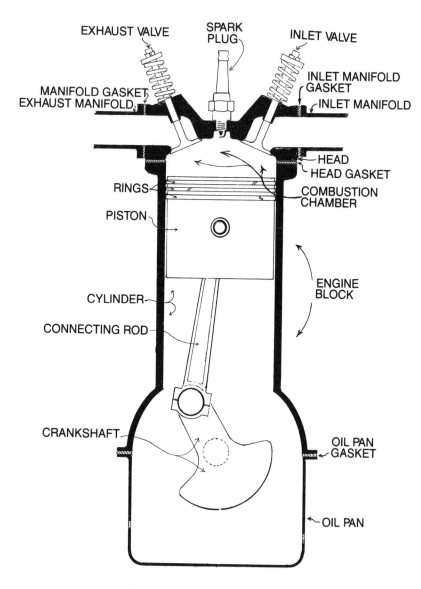

DIAGRAM A—A SINGLE COMBUSTION CHAMBER

"work." The explosions generated in your engine do the work of driving your car.

THE ENGINE CONSISTS OF TWO SECTIONS, *THE HEAD* AND *THE BLOCK*

(See diagram A)

The head is the upper section, bolted onto the top of the block. The **valves** that let in the air and fuel and let out the waste are located in the head. The protective, airtight seal between the head and block is called the **head gasket.** This airtight seal is necessary if compression is to take place.

The block is the bigger, heavier bottom section. It is fitted with hollow **cylinders**—four, six, or eight of them, depending upon the size of the engine. Inside each cylinder is a plunger-like part called a **piston,** which slides up and down inside the cylinder. The bottom of each piston is fitted with a **connecting rod,** which joins it to the **crankshaft,** which is geared to the **camshaft** . . .

("The hipbone connected to the thighbone . . . the thighbone connected to the kneebone . . .")

"Short blocks" and **"long blocks"** are terms you may hear. A "short block" is the "block" section of the engine only and includes the cylinders, pistons, rings, crankshaft, etc. A "long block" is the entire engine, including both block and head.

THE PARTS IN EACH CYLINDER WORK TOGETHER TO FORM A *COMBUSTION CHAMBER* —SOMETIMES CALLED A *COMPRESSION CHAMBER.*

HOW YOUR ENGINE WORKS

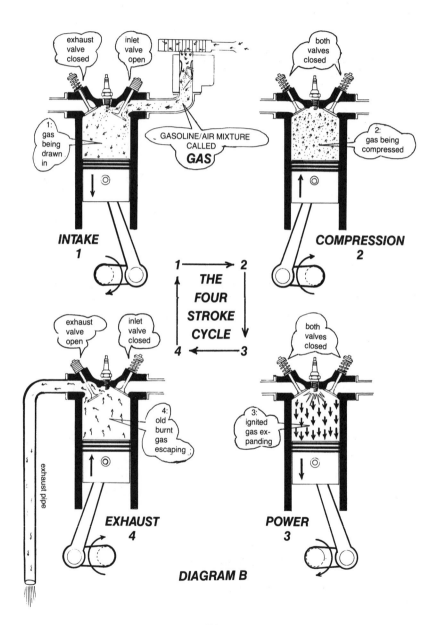

DIAGRAM B

Each piston fits into its cylinder the way a plunger fits into a hypodermic syringe. The fit is snug, but not so snug that the piston can't slide. To prevent air leakage, three or four **rings** are set into grooves in the piston's wall. As a result, two very different environments are created, one below and one above the rings. (See diagram A.)

ABOVE THE RINGS:

The combustion chamber is formed, closed off at the top by the head and head gasket. Fuel and air are fed into the chamber and then exposed to a spark from a spark plug. The spark sets off an explosion that drives the piston downward in the cylinder. This effect is called "powering."

MEANWHILE, BELOW THE RINGS:

The downward push of the piston reaches the crankshaft, making it turn. As it turns, the crankshaft forces the piston back up again, initiating a whole new cycle.

As we will explain in chapter 10, part of this same "push" is also "transmitted" (through the transmission system) to the wheels, forcing them to turn.

THE FOUR-STROKE CYCLE

The process of letting fuel into a cylinder, then having it compressed, powered, and exhausted, is called the **four-stroke cycle.** (See diagram B.)

These cycles occur in one cylinder after another in a preset **firing order,** so rapidly that the output of power is virtually continuous. Thousands of cycles are repeated each and every minute your car is driving at highway speeds.

Diagrams A and B Illustrate How the Air-Fuel Mixture Is Delivered and Waste Products Removed.

The **inlet valves** let the air-fuel mixture in. (Air only, in a fuel-injector system.) Inlet valves are preset to open as soon as a previous cycle has been completed.

The **exhaust valves** allow the waste products to escape. Each time the piston is pushed up, it forces out whatever may have been present in the chamber.

It all works very much like breathing or digestion. We take in our air and fuel, "burn" what we need, then eliminate the waste.

To Summarize the Four-Stroke Cycle:

Air and fuel are fed into the combustion chambers in preset order, compressed, and ignited. The resulting explosions push the pistons down into the cylinders. The action of the pistons turns the crankshaft, which passes this motion on to the wheels.

The turning of the crankshaft also pushes the pistons back up into the cylinders. Thus, waste is forced out through the exhaust valves and the whole four-stroke cycle can start over.

THE CARE AND MAINTENANCE OF ENGINES:

Engine wear cannot be prevented, but it can be slowed drastically. Today's engines are much sturdier than those of a generation ago, which were expected to need major work after 40,000 to 60,000 miles. With ideal care, modern engines last two to four times as long.

Four Simple Rules For Long Engine Life:

1) *Keep your car well tuned.* Frequent tuning assures that the engine will not have to work harder than necessary to drive the car.

2) *Check oil frequently and change it often. Change the oil filter as well.* Metal parts wear when they rub together. Oil coats these parts and protects them, but dirty, gritty oil will add to the friction rather than preventing it.

3) *Always warm up a cold car (allow it to idle) before driving,* even in good weather when the car starts readily. Two minutes of idling gives the oil a chance to circulate through the engine and prevent "lubrication starvation."

4) *Follow the recommended maintenance schedules in your owner's manual.*

See also the maintenance lists in the Appendix.

ENGINE WORK IS NOTORIOUSLY (AND UNAVOIDABLY) EXPENSIVE.

To get at an engine's interior, mechanics must entirely remove other systems, then later put them back. This takes hours of labor. Also, engine parts must be fitted together just so, which requires extensive grinding and adjusting, adding on more hours.

Fortunately, engine trouble serious enough to require major work is not a frequent event. Also, most engine problems come on gradually, so your annual diagnostic tests will usually give you warning.

When Rings Wear:

Compression weakens some oil escapes into the combustion chamber, where it is burned. As a result, gradually and over time:

- Performance goes down.
- Fuel consumption goes up.
- The car requires progressively more oil.
- The engine begins to "misfire" or "miss."
- Blue smoke comes from the exhaust.

When Valves Wear:

Air leaks begin to develop, and unburned fuel starts to escape, causing similar problems as with rings, with the exception that much less excess oil is burned.

MOST ENGINE TROUBLES DEVELOP SLOWLY AND CAN BE LIVED WITH A LONG TIME.

Don't feel you have to trade your car in or rush into expensive repairs at the first sign of increased oil consumption or decreased performance. Cars in the early stages of engine wear may still give many months or even years of useful service.

SOMETIMES ENGINE PROBLEMS ARE DIFFICULT TO DIAGNOSE.

As we have seen, many automotive troubles are quickly

diagnosed through simple processes of elimination. Engine problems, however, are more complicated.

PROBLEMS IN OTHER SYSTEMS CAN MIMIC ENGINE PROBLEMS:

Faulty ignition, loose carburetor hold-down nuts, bad gas, the wrong type of oil, problems with the exhaust system, even poor driving habits can result in problems similar to those caused by malfunctioning engines.

Since these minor conditions are common and also cheap to correct, have them checked out before jumping to the conclusion that you have engine trouble.

A COMPRESSION TEST WILL SHOW WHETHER THE PROBLEM IS IN THE CYLINDERS.

The mechanic removes the spark plugs, operates the starter switch, and uses a gauge that measures the pounds-per-square-inch of pressure within each cylinder.

This procedure takes from ten minutes to an hour or more, depending on the make and model of your car, the number of cylinders, and the competence and/or greed of your mechanic. Expect to pay between $15 and $50. This test can be done at almost any service facility or as part of a larger checkup at a diagnostic center.

The numbers will tell the story. Cylinders in good condition will have compression readings between about 140 and 180 pounds-per-square-inch, although this range will vary somewhat for different makes. Any compression reading below 100 indicates serious problems.

If only one cylinder measures very low while the others are normal, the trouble is localized in that particular cylinder. Perhaps one valve is sticking or damaged or one ring broken.

Abnormally low readings in two adjacent cylinders only may indicate two defective cylinders. More likely, though, it means that the head gasket has been "blown"—that is, has sprung a leak—between those two cylinders. (More about "head gaskets" shortly.)

Marginal or low readings in most or all cylinders means that the problem is general and deteriorating and that extensive valve and/or ring work is needed.

MECHANICS CAN USUALLY PINPOINT WHETHER THE TROUBLE IS IN THE VALVES OR THE RINGS EVEN WITHOUT FANCY EQUIPMENT.

In a "wet test," for instance, a bit of oil is injected into the spark plug hole of the cylinder in question, then the compression test is repeated. If the reading improves, it indicates that the rings are the problem. If there is no change, the valves are indicated.

There are more sophisticated tests than this. The point is that pinpointing the problem is not a huge task.

IF ONLY A VALVE JOB IS INDICATED, DON'T BE TALKED INTO GETTING A RING JOB TOO.

Drivers are often persuaded to do the rings as a "preventive measure," to avoid trouble "down the road." But "down the road" may be 50,000 miles away. Valves fail far more often than rings. So, unless your car is burning a lot of oil, assume that the rings are okay. Why triple your present costs (and your mechanic's profits) just to "prevent" something that may never happen?

You'd probably be smarter not to put your valve job in the hands of a mechanic who tries to scare you about the rings. He's the kind who is likely to leave something undone or to deliberately do something wrong just to be able to say *I told you so,* and to force you into a separate and probably fraudulent ring job.

VALVE JOBS:

Usually, a valve job consists of "refacing" the valves, then grinding the valves and the "valve seats" into a "mating fit." If any valve is badly worn or bent it will have to be replaced with a new one. Grinding will still be required to create the fit.

If only one valve is faulty—stuck or broken, for example— and the car is fairly new, it makes sense to have only that one valve done. In general, however—certainly if the car has done over 40,000 miles—it's better to do them all.

Count on about forty-five minutes of labor time for the valves feeding each cylinder, plus two to six hours more for opening up and reassembling the engine, depending on engine size and structure and how many extra systems such as air conditioners, turbos, or fuel injectors must be cleared out of the way. Check with the *Chilton Guide* for a maximum estimated time for your own make and model. If new parts are required, check their prices, then apply the FAIR PRICE FORMULA.

A new head gasket should always be put in after valve work.

ABOUT HEAD GASKETS:

Mechanics will try to cause panic by telling you in ominous tones that "your head gasket has been blown." What this really means is that the thin seal between the block and head has sprung a leak. The primary symptom will be noisy, regular misfiring.

The important thing to remember is that *the blowing of a head gasket cannot damage the engine.* It is not caused by malfunctioning cylinders and does not require any work on the cylinders, but it must be replaced right away.

Head gasket-blowing problems can be caused by the head and block being improperly fitted. If so, the next time a new gasket is fitted, proper head tightening procedures should be practiced. Also, impatient drivers who rev up or accelerate or drive too fast tend to build up the kind of pressures that can blow the gasket.

One simple way to test the condition of the head gasket is to fill the radiator to the top, turn on the engine, then look to see whether bubbles of air rise up into the radiator. If they do, then there must be a leak in the gasket letting air into the cooling system. Anyone who says that engines must be taken apart to check gasket condition is not to be trusted.

Replacement of the head gasket takes from three to seven hours, depending on car design and how many systems such as air conditioners or turborchargers will have to be removed and replaced. Check maximum allowable time for your model with *Chilton* and use your FAIR PRICE FORMULA. Head gaskets themselves cost around $25. Check the price for your own model.

Head gaskets should always be replaced—even if they seem

in good condition—any time they are removed for any reason.

RING JOBS:

Ring jobs are more involved and expensive than valve jobs because they require the mechanic to "go down into the block." Worn rings must be replaced by new ones and then fitted to the piston and cylinders.

Ring jobs should include replacement of the connecting rod bearings. If rings have worn out, bearings almost surely have too. Very badly worn bearings cause a banging sound. When that happens, you are in a critical situation. The car could stop dead at any time.

PROBLEMS IN THE BLOCK ARE HARD TO PREDICT:

The mechanic can't always know what he will find until he finds it. Tests can't always tell him either. Pistons and/or cylinders may prove to be too worn to accept new rings. The crankshaft may also be in poor condition.

In engines that legitimately need a "valves-rings-and-bearings job," such complications may well occur. For that reason, you may decide on a complete overhaul or rebuilding job from the start. The expense of "going into the block" is so great to begin with that it makes a kind of sense to get everything possible done and start fresh with the equivalent of a brand-new engine.

OVERHAULS AND REBUILDING JOBS:

Minor overhaul is a term often used for valve-and-ring jobs.

Bearings may or may not be included. Usually, the mechanic goes in and finds (or claims to find) further problems. Such problems could turn out to be endless.

Major overhaul is a term often used for the renewal and/or replacement of all engine parts. Cylinders are "re-bored" and fitted with new, slightly larger pistons and rings. The shaft is reground and fitted with slightly smaller bearings. All the valves are reground or replaced with new valves, which also have to be ground. The result is an engine more powerful than it was when new.

A major overhaul takes a full working week, or more. An engine that has been given a major overhaul is said to have been "rebuilt."

Installation of a rebuilt engine consists of taking out the original engine and replacing it with one that has been factory rebuilt. The housing will have been renewed and all working parts either renewed or replaced. This sort of replacement job takes one or two days.

Overhauls Versus Installations of Rebuilt Engines:

There is a definite trend toward installing factory-rebuilt engines rather than overhauling or rebuilding engines in the shop.

Busy mechanics prefer installations because they take less time, require less skill, and produce more profit. Car owners prefer them because of the better quality control and the fact that they get the car back sooner. Whichever you choose, however, make sure that you get a list of every part and procedure done, that this list covers the bearings, pistons, cylinders, and crankshaft, and that all of it is guaranteed.

What Overhauls and Replacements Cost:

Prices are high and a bit flaky. On one recent day in San Francisco, we sought quotes from four engine specialists for overhauling a 1979 4-cylinder Chevette with air conditioning but no other special features. The prices quoted were $1,054, $1,860, $1,954, and "about $1,900."

For installing a remanufactured engine in this same car, the quotations from the same sources were $2,121, $1,928, $1,995, and "under $2,000." (Prices for a bigger, more elaborate engine would have been higher.)

Obviously, the $1,054 figure for overhauling would seem the best buy. But on closer questioning, this company confessed that by an *overhaul* they meant *only a ring and valve job*. We also learned that taking out and replacing the air conditioning unit would add another $75. Adding on their prices for reboring the cylinders, regrinding the crankshaft, replacing the pistons, etc., we soon saw that installing a remanufactured engine at $1,928 would be cheaper in the long run.

These are the sorts of problems you will be faced with, too. When getting quotes for engine work, you must be sure precisely what is meant by the terms each mechanic uses.

AT SUCH PRICES, CAN OVERHAULING OR REBUILDING BE WORTH IT?

Most cars that need rebuilt engines are too old to have much market value. Even in perfect condition, our theoretical Chevette would not be worth the $2,000 it would take to fix it.

Yet replacement value can be more important than market value. A rebuilt engine promises between 100,000 to 200,000 miles of service. Only a brand-new car promises as much. The $2,000 dollar price would scarcely cover the sales tax, registration, and extra insurance on a new car, never mind the price of the car itself. Also, you would not find a used car for sale for $2,000 with a guaranteed good-as-new engine.

What it comes down to is whether you like your car enough to keep it and whether it is otherwise in good condition.

LESSER ENGINE PROBLEMS:

Detonation (also called "knocking") is that rattling noise you hear when you climb a steep hill or speed up quickly. It is caused by the too-rapid burning of inferior fuel during the combustion process. The leaded gas of yesteryear was of higher octane than fuels used today and also contained "antiknock" additives that are now lacking. Detonation is relatively harmless but will damage pistons over the very long run. To reduce it to a minimum, downshift for climbing and use the highest octane, highest quality gas available.

Preignition is characterized by a loss of power under stressful conditions (uphill driving or heavy loads), sometimes accompanied by "pinging." This problem will not show up on the compression test. What is happening is that the buildup of carbon in an older engine causes hot spots, which causes the fuel to ignite prematurely. Detergent additives and/or fuels will sometimes dissolve these deposits and should be tried. If they fail, the carbon will have to be scraped out by hand. Scraping can take from five to ten hours, depending on the engine's size and accessibility and how much carbon has built up. Have your mechanic explain his time estimate and apply the FAIR PRICE FORMULA.

Tappet noises are caused when the tappets (which regulate the opening and the closing of the valves) have gotten out of adjustment. "Adjusting the clearance" is a one-to-two-hour job and requires no new parts. However, if the car is approaching the 100,000-mile mark, the tappets may have worn and need "renewing." This is a bigger job, taking three to four hours or more, depending on the size and accessibility of your engine.

SITUATIONS IN WHICH IT IS NOT LIKELY THAT THE ENGINE IS AT FAULT:

If performance is fine but you start using more oil than in the past, you may need a different weight of oil or you may have a slow leak. Look beneath the front of the car to see whether a dirty-looking smear is collecting on the underside.

If your car suddenly loses power or stops dead on the road, suspect a loose electrical connection, or a blockage in the fuel line, or vapor lock, or being out of fuel. If you get an overheating signal, suspect a broken fanbelt.

If steam suddenly starts pouring out from under the hood, most likely a radiator hose has sprung a leak and soaked the spark plugs.

A short period of overheating almost never damages an engine. (To prevent damage, of course, you should be aware of your warning signal and stop as quickly as is safe and feasible, to let the engine cool.)

TO SUM UP:

THE "BLOCK" IS THE BOTTOM SECTION OF THE ENGINE,

CONTAINING THE CYLINDERS, PISTONS, RINGS, CON-NECTING RODS AND CRANKSHAFT.

THE "HEAD" IS THE UPPER SECTION OF THE ENGINE, CON-TAINING THE INLET AND EXHAUST (OUTLET) VALVES.

THE "HEAD GASKET" FORMS AN AIRTIGHT SEAL BETWEEN HEAD AND BLOCK, SO THAT COMPRESSION CAN TAKE PLACE WITHIN THE COMBUSTION CHAMBERS FORMED IN THE CYLINDERS.

THE "FOUR-STROKE-CYCLE" TAKES PLACE IN THE CYLIN-DERS. THE AIR-FUEL MIX IS FED IN AND IGNITED BY SPARKS IN A PRESET ORDER. THE PISTONS ARE FORCED DOWN THE CYLINDERS, CREATING A MOVEMENT IN THE CRANK-SHAFT THAT IS TRANSMITTED TO THE WHEELS OF THE CAR. THE CRANKSHAFT FORCES THE PISTONS UP AGAIN TO DRIVE OUT THE WASTE. THE CYCLE IS THEN REPEATED.

CONSISTENT MAINTENANCE, INCLUDING OIL CHANGES, "WARMING UP" BEFORE DRIVING, AND FREQUENT TUNE-UPS, WILL GREATLY EXTEND ENGINE LIFE.

PROPERLY MAINTAINED CARS CAN GO UPWARD OF 100,000 MILES BEFORE ENGINE WEAR BECOMES SERIOUS AND SYMPTOMATIC.

MOST ENGINE SYMPTOMS DEVELOP SLOWLY AND DO NOT CREATE EMERGENCIES.

COMPRESSION TESTS ACCURATELY GAUGE THE HEALTH OF THE CYLINDERS.

ONCE OVERHAULED OR REBUILT, ENGINES ARE AS GOOD AS NEW.

10

The Transmission System

THE TRANSMISSION SYSTEM DELIVERS THE POWER CREATED BY THE ENGINE TO THE WHEELS, BOOSTING OR REDUCING POWER AS NEEDED.

"Transmission" comes from two Latin roots that mean "send across." As part of the "drive train" that converts explosions in the cylinders into useful power, its job is to *send* the power *across*.

To illustrate, we'll forget about cars for a moment and consider bicycles.

In a Bicycle:

The rider takes the place of the engine. He supplies his own

POWER AND TRANSMISSION

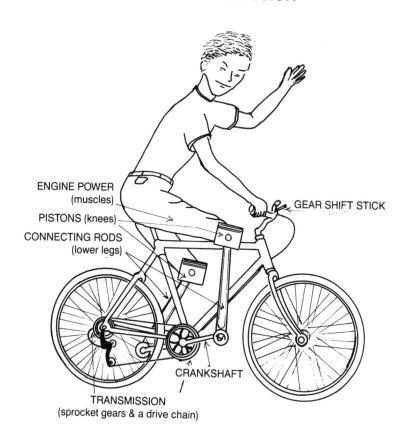

ENGINE POWER (muscles)

PISTONS (knees)

CONNECTING RODS (lower legs)

GEAR SHIFT STICK

CRANKSHAFT

TRANSMISSION
(sprocket gears & a drive chain)

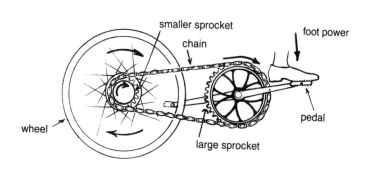

smaller sprocket

chain

foot power

wheel

large sprocket

pedal

power to drive the wheels. He does this by pumping the pedals with his feet.

Look at our illustration. You will see how the chain connects the pedals to the rear wheel. The chain is the means by which the rider's energy is "sent across."

Look again and observe how the end of the chain nearest the pedals is meshed with a large *SPROCKET* (a sort of wheel with teeth), while the other end is meshed with the smaller sprocket mounted on the rear wheel.

As a result, when the rider pushes down on a pedal, the large sprocket is turned,

—which turns the chain,
—which turns the small sprocket,
—which turns the rear wheel.

IF YOU UNDERSTAND THAT SIMPLE SEQUENCE, THEN YOU UNDERSTAND *TRANSMISSION*.

(And you also understand why you can't ride a bike with a broken chain.)

Let's observe our bicycle one more time, and let's also assume it's a ten-speed:

The sprockets would now come with ten **gears** of different sizes—a gear being simply a toothed wheel that meshes with some other part.

The size of each gear determines how many times it will turn given the same amount of "push." The smaller a gear, the harder it is to turn, and the larger a gear, the easier it is to turn.

Depending on road conditions, a rider will often feel the need to "shift into another gear"—or "change speeds."

Shifting detaches the chain from one gear to another that is bigger or smaller. The rider shifts in order to make the best use of his energy—to have more power and control on hills, for example, or to coast easily on flat, open stretches.

HOW THIS SAME PRINCIPLE WORKS IN YOUR CAR:

In a car, of course, the engine supplies the power, not the driver. But the transmission of the energy is done much the same.

The Function of the Crankshaft:

When the engine first starts up, the engine's crankshaft has practically no energy behind it—certainly not enough to move a weighty vehicle like a car. Yet once it gets going, that same crankshaft can turn an engine over and over as many as 5,000 times per minute. Just imagine what would happen if all that motion were transferred directly to the wheels! Cars would have to be launched from Cape Canaveral.

The Flywheel Stores the Excess Energy:

Flywheels have the capacity to pass on some energy at once, while conserving the rest for later. This sort of continuity of energy is called "momentum." It's momentum that keeps your car moving steadily and smoothly, instead of in hops and jumps.

The Transmission System Regulates the Speed:

How it does this depends on whether the transmission is of the standard manual ("stick shift") kind or an automatic.

STANDARD MANUAL TRANSMISSION:

When you depress the **clutch** and shift from neutral into a gear, a set of **shifter forks** slide along the **shifter rail** inside the transmission, until it arrives at the chosen gear.

When you then release the clutch, the chosen gear engages with the rest of the transmission, passing along the power to the wheels.

All these parts through which the engine's power is transmitted are called the **drive train** or **power train.**

IN A REAR-WHEEL DRIVE (RWD):

The transmission turns the **differential** (part of the **rear axle**), which turns the **rear wheels**; which "push" or "drive" the car. Rear-wheel drive is traditional and many older cars still have it.

IN A FRONT-WHEEL DRIVE (FWD):

The transmission turns the **transaxle,** which drives the **front wheels,** which "pull" the car. Front-wheel drive gives better mileage and handling and has virtually become standard.

THERE ARE ALSO SEVERAL VARIETIES OF FOUR-WHEEL DRIVES (4WD):

Some are basically rear-wheel drive systems, with additional mechanism to engage the front wheels when required. Others are essentially front-wheel drive systems with means to activate the rear wheels. Some are automatic, triggered by any need for greater traction, while others require the driver to use a switch. Four-wheel drive enhances safety, maneuverability, and handling, but costs a premium to buy, fuel, and repair. At present, only about one percent of new cars have it, but its popularity is growing fast.

The Clutch:

The clutch "engages" and "disengages" the drive line. That is,

THE DRIVE TRAIN (STANDARD TRANSMISSION)

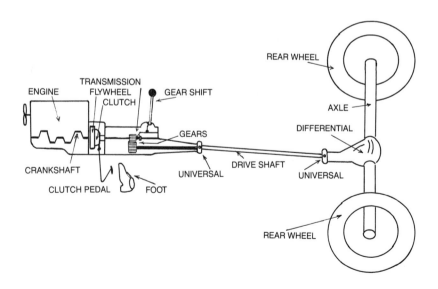

it hooks the engine to the transmission and then unhooks it again.

An unhooked engine keeps turning over without moving the car. There are times when this is necessary—such as during warming up or idling in traffic. The engine also must be unhooked when shifting from one gear to another.

Each time you step on the clutch pedal, you unhook the engine. Each time you put your car into neutral, you keep it disengaged until you shift again. And every time you shift from one gear to another, you have to go through the neutral position.

The Stick (or "Manual Shift" or "Gear-Shift Lever):

Use of manual shifting allows the driver to choose whichever gear seems best for the circumstances, just the way the bike rider would do.

Gears are lined up according to their "gear ratios"—that is, in relation to how many revolutions each gear makes each time the crankshaft turns. We talk about "shifting up" to a "higher gear" or "shifting down" to a "lower" one.

Torque is the energy needed to cause a rotation. When an engine is just starting up, or is running at low speed, it produces very little torque. So the driver puts the car in a "low gear" to make the most of what little torque is available.

A car using a low gear to get started requires a lot of energy to move it—just as a bike rider has to push extra hard to get his bike going. But once a vehicle picks up speed, it produces more torque. The driver can shift into high gear and let the engine cruise along, thereby using less fuel.

This is the reason you get better fuel mileage on the highway than in city traffic, even though you're driving so much faster.

You should not skip gears in shifting—such as going from first to fourth. When you do, you ask the transmission to change its motion faster than it can handle, and the gears won't "mesh" properly. Damage can result.

Standard Transmission Systems Are Meant to Last For the Lifetime of the Car—If They're Not Abused.

Unfortunately, it's easy to abuse them. They almost seem to invite it. For example, the most safe-feeling way to hold a stick-shift car when you have to stop or idle while climbing is to shift into first gear, then play with the partial engagement of the clutch. In a city like San Francisco, with its steep hills, this technique is necessary—which is why the city is known to be "murder on clutches."

Many drivers play with the clutch this way not only on hills but every time they have to idle in traffic. Nothing will wear out a clutch faster.

Whenever possible, do your idling in neutral and rely on your foot and hand brakes to hold your car. Shift into gear only when free to move again.

Most Forms of Clutch Abuse Are Unconscious and Unintended:

Riding the clutch: Some drivers habitually rest the left foot on the clutch pedal while driving along. *Don't!*

Driving with the clutch out of adjustment: Clutches should be set to allow an inch or two of free play before engagement takes place. This prevents accidental disengagement or excessive wear. With too little free play, clutches feels stiff and shifting is jolting and jerky. With too much free play, clutches feel "mushy" or "spongy" and gears will not shift well.

Clutch Slippage:

Habitual abuse wears out the lining of the clutch plate, leading to "clutch slippage." When clutches slip, one or more of your gears may not always engage properly on the first try. You may have to shift a second time to get a response.

An **adjustment** will sometimes help. Clutches are made so they can be tightened several times. The job takes only about 15 to 25 minutes and require no parts. According to THE FAIR PRICE FORMULA, it should cost between $12 and $20, but we've been quoted a flat $30 in expensive San Francisco. A handy friend might do it for a cold beer.

If the clutch won't take an adjustment, you will need a "clutch job." The entire clutch mechanism—including clutch pressure plate, disc, and clutch-release bearing—should all be replaced. Phone a parts store and get the prices for the parts listed in your estimate. Then use the FAIR PRICE FORMULA to compare.

Some mechanics include the "refacing" of the flywheel into the job, whereas others charge extra. Be sure you ask whether the flywheel is included in any estimate and have it stated in writing.

Clutch repair runs into serious money, costing between $250 and $500, parts and labor included, for most makes. *It is very definitely a shop-around job.*

Call up dealerships, independent mechanics and franchises, chains, and independent specialists. Remember that half an hour on the phone could save you $200.

When pricing a clutch job for this book in San Francisco, we were given estimates ranging from $300 to $450. The $450 was from a dealership and didn't even include refacing the flywheel. The $300 was from a well-established transmission specialist across town and included the flywheel. We finally had the job done very satisfactorily (flywheel and all) at a

THE DRIVE TRAIN (AUTOMATIC TRANSMISSION)

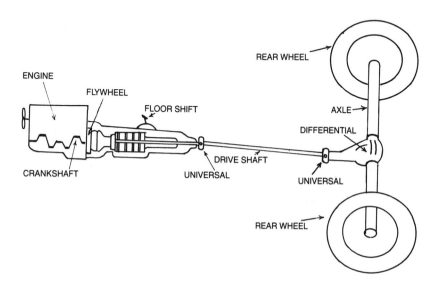

near-by chain for $325. The convenience of getting the work done in one day and close to home was worth the extra $25.

A Noisy, Sticking Clutch Indicates Trouble with One of the Bearings:

There are two bearings: the "input-shaft" bearing and the "clutch-release" bearing. The price of fixing either varies greatly according to the design of your make of car. With most imports, Fords, and GM models, expect to pay somewhere between $100 to $200. Some Chrysler-made cars can be done for as little as $40. You can figure $5–$25 for parts and one to three hours for labor. Check your estimates against the FAIR PRICE FORMULA and *Chilton.*

AUTOMATIC TRANSMISSIONS:

Like manual transmissions, automatics transfer energy to the wheels by means of gears. Most of the time, however, the transmission system—not the driver—chooses the gear.

The mechanism is also somewhat different. Instead of having forks that slide on a rail and then engage a gear, the automatic keeps all the gears engaged all the time, but prevents some from turning while letting others turn.

In Most Automatics, Connections Are Made Hydrolically.

That is, connections are made by using fluid under pressure to apply force. *Running out of fluid is the very worst thing that can happen to your automatic.* Check your transmission fluid regularly, keeping it clean and full. If the fluid starts going down faster than previously, suspect a leak and get to a mechanic fast.

Dirty Automatic Valves:

Dirt is as harmful to the automatic transmission as to any other system. Once in the automatic's valves, it causes jerky or delayed shifting. Good maintenance will tend to prevent this condition. **Valve body cleaning** takes two to three hours of labor, plus $15 to $25 for fresh transmission oil and a new oil-pan gasket. Ford and Chrysler cars tend to take longer than GM and many foreign makes. According to the FAIR PRICE FORMULA, expect totals between about $100 and $160, depending on where you live and what you drive.

Lock-Up Torque Converters:

Some late-model automatics feature this mechanism, which helps to prevent slippage and improve mileage but has the drawback of causing rather jerky acceleration when climbing. If your car has such a converter, rest assured that the jerkiness is a characteristic and not a malfunction.

Expect to Overhaul or Replace Your Automatic Transmission During the Normal Lifetime of Your Car.

This is just a fact of life. Automatic transmission does not have the longevity of engines.

Because of the difficulty of transmission work, the trend is toward replacement. Both franchised chains and the bigger independent specialists keep new and rebuilt transmissions in stock. They pop out the old and install the new for set prices starting around $400. Shop around among the transmission chains and specialists for the best deal for your make and model.

Regular Servicing Will Delay and Sometimes Prevent an Overhaul:

Service consists of draining and cleaning the system, checking for leaks, replacing transmission oil and the oil-pan gasket, and giving the car a test drive.

The cost can run between $25 and $50, depending on make, model, and location. But chains and specialty transmission shops may offer "one-price-for-all" at around $20 to $25.

TO SUM UP:

TRANSMISSIONS USE GEARS TO REGULATE THE AMOUNT OF POWER SENT FROM THE ENGINE TO THE WHEELS.

STANDARD MANUAL TRANSMISSIONS LEAVE THE CHOICE OF GEARS TO THE DRIVER.

TO INSURE LONG CLUTCH LIFE IN STANDARD TRANSMISSIONS:

- DON'T IDLE WITH THE CAR IN GEAR
- DON'T RIDE THE CLUTCH
- HAVE THE CLUTCH ADJUSTED TO ALLOW AN INCH OF FREE PLAY
- HEED ALL INSTRUCTIONS IN YOUR OWNER'S MANUAL

AUTOMATIC TRANSMISSIONS SELECT GEARS FOR THE

HOW TO KEEP YOUR CAR MECHANIC HONEST

DRIVER AND ARE EXPECTED TO REQUIRE AT LEAST ONE OVERHAUL DURING THE LIFETIME OF THE CAR.

TO PROLONG THE LIFE OF AN AUTOMATIC TRANS-MISSION:

- KEEP FLUID CLEAN AND FULL
- SERVICE REGULARLY AND ON TIME
- WATCH OUT FOR LEAKS AND REPAIR THEM AT ONCE
- HAVE VALVES CLEANED WHEN NEEDED

11

The Steering System

THE STEERING SYSTEM DETERMINES THE DIRECTION IN WHICH THE WHEELS WILL GO.

This will be a very short chapter for a very pleasant reason. Steering systems are virtually indestructible and seldom need attention. Since your goal is to know only enough to communicate effectively with your mechanic, you need know little about the steering system.

Most "steering" problems are caused by the tires or wheel alignment—which we will discuss in chapter 18, The Suspension System.

To give you a nodding acquaintance with steering systems, we will describe the three most common types. Of these, only "power steering" tends to cause occasional problems.

STANDARD MANUAL STEERING:

Turning the **steering wheel** turns the **steering column** (or "shaft"), which is joined within the **steering box** to a **worm gear** screwed into a big **nut** with a whole lot of **ball bearings.** These reduce friction and cause the rotation of the **pitman shaft and arm** (a joint and short rod), which pass the movement on to a series of **ball joints** to the **relay tie rod,** the **steering arms,** and the **steering knuckles**—which actually turn the front wheels.

THE STEERING SYSTEM

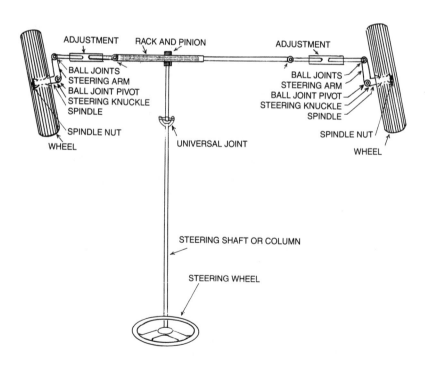

"RACK-AND-PINION" STEERING:

This is a simple system, in which the turning of the **steering column** and **universal joint** rotates a **gear** that is crossed by and meshed with the **rack**. The rack is extended to the right and left to join **ball joints** connected to **steering arms, steering knuckles,** and **spindles,** on which the front wheels are fitted. (See illustration.)

"Rack and pinion" is a simpler, more direct method of steering, allowing more sensitive and precise control; but since it calls for more effort from the driver, it is used mainly in light, small cars. Powered systems are now being introduced.

POWER STEERING:

This method provides a boost to standard manual systems, and is especially helpful for parallel parking. **A pump drives fluid under pressure** into the steering box, through **rotary valves.** The pressure moves a **piston,** which moves the **nut,** which rotates the **pitman shaft,** and so forth.

Problems Connected with Power Steering:

If steering feels soft and there is too much free play, check the level of the power-steering fluid.

If the level is not down, you probably need an "adjustment" at about $15.

If the level is down, add more fluid and also have the hoses checked for leaks. If defective, a power steering hose costs between $20 and $40 to replace—imports and GMs being the more costly; a pressure hose costs about twice as much.

Changing the hose takes only a couple of minutes. Call a parts store for the price of the needed hose for your own make and models.

If steering is still unresponsive and there are leaks and the car is really old, the power steering will have to be overhauled. This is a three to five hour job, costing about an average of $200, (plus or minus $50) depending on make and model. Or you may have to replace the power steering pump, which costs around the same. Check out the parts prices and *Chilton* time estimates for your model and use the FAIR PRICE FORMULA.

Make sure the mechanic locates the exact source of any leak before he begins work, so he knows which job to do. Any defect in the power steering creates much the same sensations of softness and too much free play, so the primary means of diagnosis is to track down the leak.

If your power steering "screams" when you make a sharp turn in either direction, your power steering belt needs tightening. If worn or shiny, it should be replaced with a new one, which can take from five minutes to half an hour. New belts cost under $10. Check around for labor costs—some places don't charge.

TO SUM UP:

MOST "STEERING PROBLEMS" ARE REALLY TIRE OR WHEEL ALIGNMENT PROBLEMS, WHICH WILL BE COVERED IN CHAPTER 18.

IF YOU HAVE POWER STEERING, BE ALERT TO FLUID LEVEL, BELT CONDITION, AND LEAKS.

12

The Braking System

THE BRAKING SYSTEM SLOWS, STOPS, AND LOCKS THE CAR INTO PLACE.

Any time you step on your brake pedal, you must have at your disposal enough force to control and stop a ton or two of vehicle hurtling along at the speed limit or above. In fact, it takes more force to stop a car than to get it going.

Obviously, all this force cannot come from you. It has to be created by the braking system.

No system is more important. You would be much better off if your car never started at all, than if it started but could not be slowed or stopped.

DRUM BRAKES AND DISC BRAKES:

Most cars use a combination of two braking systems—"drum brakes" in the rear and "disc brakes" up front.

How Drum Brakes Work:

Each time you step on the **brake pedal,** you apply pressure to a **piston** in the **master brake cylinder.** This in turn puts pressure on **springs,** which force brake fluid along **tubes** or **lines** to a pair of **pistons** in each **hydraulic wheel cylinder.** These two pistons transmit the pressure to a pair of **brake**

THE BRAKING SYSTEM

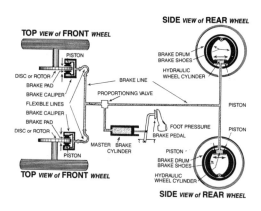

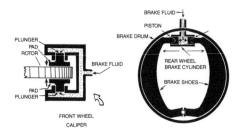

"shoes," which press out against **rotating "drums"** on the rear wheels, forcing them to a halt.

This is a system that uses a tremendous amount of friction. As a result, drum brakes wear out fast.

How Disc Brakes Work:

Stepping on the **brake pedal** also puts pressure on the **master cylinder,** which then forces some of the **brake fluid** along to **pistons** on the front wheels. These pistons apply pressure to the **hydrolic brake caliper,** which tightens the two **pads** sandwiched around the **disc** (or **"rotor"**) that turns with each wheel. The pressure of the pads stops the wheel.

Disc brakes use less friction than drum brakes. They apply pressure to a much smaller area of the wheel, which means less heat is built up. Also, disc brakes dry faster under wet conditions. All these factors make them longer lasting and more reliable than drum brakes.

Disc brakes are always put up front because 75% of braking action occurs up front. Racing models and a few sports cars use disc brakes on all four wheels. In fact, disc brakes were invented for use on racing cars.

Why Use Drum Brakes At All?

1) **For added safety.** Used in combination, the drum brakes back up disc brakes. Hydrolic systems can spring leaks, which could be disastrous in a braking system. (Racing cars, of course, are serviced constantly, so most potential disc-brake danger is averted.)

2) **Because they can also be used as parking brakes.**

PARKING BRAKES (OR "HAND BRAKES" OR "EMERGENCY BRAKES"):

In most cars, when you "pull your hand brake" (or step on your "parking brake") you pull on a **cable** that forces the **brake shoes** against the **rear brake drums**.

When your parking brake loosens, it can be "tightened" in a few minutes by adjusting the cable. You should be able to find someone to do this for you for under $10. *There is no more important safety precaution than keeping this brake tight.*

Your Parking Brake Is Your Insurance, Your Lifesaver.

If your pedal system fails, you can use your handbrake to stop your car, then to brake it until you can get to the nearest service station.

POWER BRAKES:

Some cars feature a vacuum-powered booster to increase pressures. This eases braking, especially on large, heavy cars.

MAINTAINING BRAKING SYSTEMS:

Since all brake systems use friction, wear is inevitable. You can slow it down but not prevent it. So take brake maintenance seriously. It costs less to maintain discs and drums than to cure smashed heads and bodies.

Avoid braking hard. Slamming on the brakes abuses and taxes them. That "scream" you hear is *pain!*

Keep alert. Watch for such symptoms as a mushy rather than firm feel to the pedal, any pull to the left or right as you brake, (which can also be caused by tire and suspension problems), and any lack of resistence when you push the pedal to the floor.

Don't ride the brakes. Keep your foot off the brake while driving. (Some drivers keep it on quite unconsciously.) And always make sure your parking brake is disengaged while you drive.

Have brakes inspected at least twice a year. Brake pads and linings wear so gradually that you may not notice anything until you suddenly hear that scream of metal against metal and discover your brakes are "gone." Brakes should be "relined" as soon as linings have reached certain measurable conditions of wear.

REPAIRS TO THE BRAKE SYSTEM:

If you find your wheels skidding or your tail occasionally in the air on stops, have the *proportioning valve* checked and replaced if necessary. (The proportioning valve coordinates the two sets of brakes, making sure each set gets the right amount of pressure so they will slow down and stop together.)

This job (much more common in front-wheel-drive cars) takes under an hour. Make sure the mechanic puts in only the valve for your make, model, and year. Check out the price of the valve and apply the FAIR PRICE FORMULA.

If the pedal gets too low and soft, have the drum brakes "adjusted." This is a flat fee job, taking under half-an-hour and requiring no parts. Expect to pay between $13 and $20, depending on where you live.

If the feel of the brake is mushy but the adjustment looks okay, air may have gotten into the system, replacing some of the brake fluid. If brake fluid was too low or too dirty, "bleeding the brakes" will correct the problem.

Bleeding the Brakes consists of adding more brake fluid to the master cylinder reservoir, then letting out the excess fluid and air from the wheels, one at a time. Bleeding takes about thirty minutes and averages about $20—less in rural areas, a bit more in the city.

Checking for Leaks:

Whenever air gets into the brake system, it is necessary to check for leaks. Brake leaks create an obvious, colorless, wettish smear. Different kinds of brake leaks have different patterns. Ask your mechanic to look for such leaks and point them out to you. (Or *you* can find them and point them out to him.)

Smears inside the tires or behind the wheels means leaks either in the brake cylinders or the flexible lines (hoses) leading to them. If there's a kind of spray all around the area, then it's more likely to be a hose.

Brake cylinders require one to two hours each to repair. (Probably only one cylinder is leaking and will need work.) If a new brake cylinder is needed, it should cost around $125 and the job upwards of an hour. Check the price of a new cylinder for your model and apply the FAIR PRICE FORMULA.

Hose (or "line") leaks are repaired by putting on a new hose. The hose costs about $20 and the job takes fifteen minutes.

A wettish smear *inside* **the car, near the brake pedal,** indicates a leak in the *master cylinder*. Master cylinders are almost invariably replaced rather than repaired. Check the price of the unit for your own model, assume one hour of labor, and apply the FAIR PRICE FORMULA. Fresh brake fluid and bleeding should be included in the job. You can save by having the work done at a chain.

Relining Jobs:

When drum brake "shoes" or disc brake "pads" wear thin, they need to be replaced. Such jobs are called "relinings."

Low brake pedal and insecure stopping indicates worn **drum shoes.** Shoes cost $25 to $35, including markup, for most models. Putting them on takes up to two hours. The bleeding and adjustment should be included in the price, as well as "cutting the drums" for refitting.

Prices differ little from make to make, averaging about $100. You can save about a third by taking advantage of the low flat rates offered by chains.

A grinding noise and difficulty in stopping indicate worn disc pads. Disc pad sets cost about $15 to $30 for most models. Putting them on takes about an hour, including "smoothing" the discs and bleeding the brakes. Substantial savings can be had at chains for this job too.

Repairs Due to Neglect Of Brakes:

When linings are allowed to wear out completely, metal parts come into contact and immediately ruin each other through friction. These parts have to be replaced. New **rotors** for disc brakes and **drums** for drum brakes cost $50 to $60 each, requiring at least half an hour each to install. Commit yourself to keeping your brakes well lined and you will never have to calculate or pay such costs.

TO SUM UP:

THE BRAKES ARE THE MOST IMPORTANT AND POWERFUL SYSTEM IN YOUR CAR.

USE THEM GENTLY AND HAVE THEM CHECKED AND SERVICED REGULARLY.

HAVE RELINING DONE LONG BEFORE METAL PARTS BECOME EXPOSED.

CHECK FOR POSSIBLE LEAKS WHENEVER THE BRAKES GET MUSHY, FLUID GETS LOW, OR BLEEDING IS REQUIRED.

13

The Generating System

LET'S PREFACE THIS CHAPTER WITH A BRIEF REVIEW.

We mentioned in the first chapter that there are three kinds of systems in an automobile:

- Systems that make the car move;
- Systems that serve and support;
- Systems that keep the rest healthy.

We have now completed our survey of the systems that make the car move. Next, we will look at the systems that serve and support, then go on to those that keep the rest healthy. The systems that serve and support are the generating system and the electrical system.

THE GENERATING SYSTEM SUPPLIES ELECTRICITY TO THE BATTERY, WHERE IT IS STORED UNTIL NEEDED BY THE ELECTRICAL SYSTEM OR BY THE OTHER SYSTEMS THAT DEPEND ON ELECTRICITY.

There's not much to the generating system—only a **battery, battery connections,** an **alternator,** and a **voltage regulator.** But nothing else could function without them.

THE BATTERY:

The battery stores energy for start-up and other purposes. It consists of a series of positively and negatively charged lead **plates,** forming **"cells"** filled with **electrolyte**—a mix of water and acid through which electic current can flow. For the

THE GENERATING SYSTEM

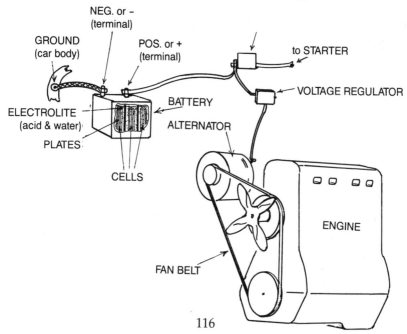

battery to work, current must flow between the **positive and negative terminals** on the top or the side of the battery.

The Battery Connections:

These are the **terminals** and the **cables,** which are attached to the terminals by **bolts.**

There are **positive and negative cables** to go with the positive and negative terminals.

- The *positive cable,* marked "+" or "pos," is attached to the positive terminal. It connects the battery to the solenoid and is usually red.

- The *negative cable,* marked "−" or "neg," is attached to the negative terminal. It connects the battery to some metal part of the car to "ground" it. It is either black or of copper braid.

The battery will not function or transmit its power unless these two cables are in good condition and are firmly attached to the matching terminals.

THE ALTERNATOR:

The alternator is the primary source of electric power while the car is running. It keeps the battery charged. The alternator is driven by the **fan belt** (part of the cooling system).

THE VOLTAGE REGULATOR:

This part adjusts the flow of electricity from the alternator, according to how much is needed by the battery.

ANOTHER BIT OF REVIEW:

In chapter 4, The Starter System, we mentioned that when the solenoid is turned on, current flows from the battery through the solenoid to the starter motor to start the car.

We also mentioned that most failures to start are caused by the battery or its connections. We suggested that if your car won't start, you try your headlights and also check whether battery cables look sound and connections are firm and clean. For the purpose of explaining the starting system, we assumed that the battery, cables, and connections all were fine.

We will now assume that the battery, cables, and connections are *not* so fine.

HOW THE BATTERY AND ITS CONNECTIONS AFFECT STARTING:

While a car is being driven, the battery collects and stores energy for the next start-up. Any time that energy fails to store, gets "drained," or is blocked from "flowing," the next start-up will fail.

Any number of things can drain a battery. The most common cause is forgetting to turn headlights off after driving. But leaving the glove compartment open or a door ajar overnight can also drain a battery.

Check for such a cause. If something has been left on, you can hope that the battery is not defective but merely "low."

GET THE CAR STARTED; THEN GET THE BATTERY CHARGED.

To do this, you must "borrow" power from another source—such as someone else's battery. You do this with the use of **booster cables,** (or "jumper leads" or "jump cords") which are used to connect your battery terminals to those of a well-charged battery. A set of cables costs between $8 and $30. They are easy to use, but be sure to follow the instructions exactly. The less expensive ones are perfectly adequate.

Invest in a set of booster cables, even if you wouldn't dare use them yourself. People willing and able to help might not happen to have a set. Your automobile club will come and give you a "boost" with their own cables, but you may have to wait an hour or longer for them to show up for a procedure that takes two minutes.

TWO WAYS OF CHARGING A BATTERY:

Once you've had your "boost," you can simply run your motor for five minutes, then drive around for half an hour. Your generator system will charge the battery. Alternatively, you get your car to a service station and let them charge it for you for about $10 or less.

If your battery won't start again next time, repeat the same procedure. You may not have charged long enough the previous time. Check again to see if some small light hasn't been left burning. If you don't have a sealed "no maintenance" battery, have the electrolyte ("water") level checked and filled up if necessary.

If the Battery Still Won't Keep a Charge:

A **circuit test** will pinpoint the failure. The circuit test covers battery, battery connections, alternator, and voltage regulator and costs about $10. (The price of the test should be deducted from the cost of whatever work proves necessary.)

IF YOU NEED A NEW BATTERY:

Don't buy more battery than you need. Buy the same size that came with the car, or whatever is recommended in your owner's manual. If in doubt, call a dealer who sells your make and ask what size he recommends.

Don't buy more time than you need. Batteries come guaranteed for anything from 12 to 60 months, or for "life." Choose something in the middle. If you are driving an older car that will be replaced within a few years, you don't need a "life" guarantee. On the other hand, batteries are too important to settle for the bottom-of-the-line.

Don't spend more than you have to. Buy from a discounter, not a service station or an auto dealer. Whenever possible, call around for prices and ask about specials. There should be no additional charge for installation.

Get a sealed (maintenance-free) battery. It will spare you having to check the electrolyte level and will pay for itself with preventive maintenance.

IF THE PROBLEM SEEMS TO BE AT THE TERMINAL CONNECTIONS:

If they look loose and you're stuck somewhere, you might try tightening the bolts yourself, either by hand or with a small wrench, then see if the car will start. As soon as you can, have a mechanic check that they are tight enough.

If one of the cables still seems loose, even if it is all right at the terminal, a mechanic will have to tighten it at the other end.

If the connections look very dirty, or corroded, they'll have to be cleaned. Since you might not care to touch them yourself, tell your mechanic to do it. A cleaning job costs between $10 and $15.

Whenever possible, watch the mechanic do these simple jobs—or have a friend show you. Learning how to do them will get you out of many an emergency.

If one of the cables looks cracked or worn, have it replaced. The cables are not costly. **Negative cables** can be replaced in a few minutes, and the total for parts and labor should come to between $15 and $30. **Positive cables** take longer, the cost varying according to the accessibility of the solenoid, to which the positive cable is attached. Expect inclusive estimates ranging from $20 to $40. You'll probably do best at a discount chain.

If a mechanic says a cable is damaged, have him show you. The damage should be something you can confirm with your own eyes.

THE VOLTAGE REGULATOR:

Defects will be discovered by a circuit test. Faulty regulators are replaced. A new one costs around $10 to $15 and can be put on in fifteen to thirty minutes. Check prices for your own model and locality and use the FAIR PRICE FORMULA.

ALTERNATORS:

There are both new and rebuilt replacements for failed alternators. Depending on your model, asking for a rebuilt one could save you from $20 to over $100. The job takes from sixty to ninety minutes, so check into the price of a rebuilt for your own model and use the FAIR PRICE FORMULA. Complete costs will run between $100 and $200.

Big cars perform better with **heavy-duty alternators.** New ones can cost $200 to $300 installed. You can save about half that for a rebuilt.

A WORD ABOUT FAN BELTS:

Although fan belts are part of the cooling system, they drive the alternator and therefore affect the generating system. Have your fan belt checked frequently for tightness and wear. If slack, have it adjusted—a minimum-price job. If worn, have it replaced—a ten minute job, plus the price of the belt, which is $4 to $10.

If the fan belt breaks while you're driving, your generator warning light will go on, indicating that there's no charge. Shortly after, you'll get another signal that the car is over-heating. *Stop immediately.*

TO SUM UP:

IF YOUR CAR WON'T START, INVESTIGATE THE BATTERY, BATTERY CONNECTIONS, AND FAN BELT FIRST.

A CIRCUIT TEST WILL LOCATE DEFECTS ANYWHERE IN THE GENERATING SYSTEM.

BUY ONLY AS MUCH BATTERY AS YOU NEED AND BUY IT FROM A CHAIN.

IF AN ALTERNATOR IS NEEDED, GET IT REBUILT, NOT NEW.

14

The Electrical System

THE ELECTRICAL SYSTEM RUNS THE IGNITION SYSTEM, THE STARTER MOTOR, AND SUCH AUXILIARIES AS LIGHTS AND SIGNALS, WINDSHIELD WIPERS, THE RADIO AND TAPE DECK, AND THE CIGARETTE LIGHTER.

Chapter 13, The Generating System, described how your car's electrical power is generated, showing how that power is transmitted from the battery through the positive cable and to the solenoid to turn on the starter motor.

Chapter 8, The Ignition System, explained how electric sparks are brought to the combustion chambers in the engine to ignite the fuel.

PROBLEMS WITH YOUR CAR'S *AUXILIARIES.*

As long as the generating system is working well, problems

with auxiliaries will be due to burned-out bulbs, worn switches, blown fuses, or shorted wiring.

Bulbs for stop lights, parking lights and turn signals eventually burn out. They are cheap and very easy to replace. A new bulb should cost between $4 and $8, labor included.

Turn signals sometimes won't flash, despite a good bulb. This means that you probably need a **flasher** at $10 to $15 for part and labor, inclusive.

Dashboard bulbs are less easy to get at than exterior bulbs, which means higher labor costs. Figure between $6 and $20 for bulb and labor. If you get a quote on the high side, comparison shop.

Headlights are obviously more costly than small bulbs, and their aim requires adjustment as part of the installation. For each new headlight, you'll pay about $25 to $30, installed. Specialized headlights on elite models may run more.

If the headlight works but the aim seems wrong, you'll need an **adjustment.** This should cost between $10 and $15 and requires no parts.

The dimmer switch is indicated if your headlights won't switch readily from low to high and/or high to low. Costs vary surprisingly for this job, depending on whether or not the switch is easily accessible. You might be quoted anything from $20 to $50. If you get a high estimate, research the price of the switch for your model, then have the mechanic account for his labor estimate. Use the FAIR PRICE FORMULA.

Blown fuses cause much the same problems as burned-out bulbs and worn-out switches. Before installing a new bulb or switch, a good mechanic will always check out the fuse that governs the wiring (or "circuit") related to that auxiliary. If blown, a fuse can be replaced for $5 or so, part and labor included.

Wiring may be shorted if one or more fuses blow repeatedly. Wiring jobs are the only really troublesome and expensive jobs associated with the electrical system. It can take hours of trial-and-error diagnostics to locate, then get at, an electrical trouble spot. There's no way the mechanic can make an accurate estimate in advance. All he can do is hunt until he finds the problem, then tell you what it will cost to fix.

If you suspect wiring problems, better take the car to a dealership or to someone advertising as a specialist in automotive electrical systems. Otherwise, you may end up going back again and again. Parts costs will be at most a few dollars. It's the labor that adds up. Luckily, wiring problems are comparatively rare, except in very old cars.

IF THE PROBLEM'S IN THE RADIO OR TAPE DECK:

See a specialist in car sound systems, or someone who specializes in radios and tape decks of your make.

TO SUM UP:

PROBLEMS WITH LIGHTS AND OTHER ELECTRICAL AUXILIARIES MAY BE DUE TO BURNED-OUT BULBS, WORN SWITCHES, FUSES, OR FAULTY WIRING.

BLOWN FUSES AND BURNED-OUT EXTERIOR LIGHT BULBS

ACCOUNT FOR MOST FAILURES AND ARE CHEAP AND EASY TO REPLACE.

REPLACEMENT OF DIMMER SWITCHES AND DASHBOARD BULBS VARY IN PRICE. COMPARISON SHOP AND USE THE *FAIR PRICE FORMULA.*

WIRING JOBS ARE DIFFICULT AND EXPENSIVE AND SHOULD BE DONE BY EXPERTS.

15

The Cooling (and Heating) System

THE COOLING SYSTEM KEEPS THE ENGINE FROM OVERHEATING—AND ALSO KEEPS THE PASSENGERS WARM IN COLD WEATHER.

Although they may share a single control panel, the cooling system and the air-conditioning system are unrelated. (Air conditioning will be discussed in a later chapter.) Your car's engine produces tremendous energy, and energy is heat. A portion of this heat is used in powering the car. Some of the excess goes out the exhaust. The cooling system must dispose of the rest.

COOLING IS SO VITAL THAT A CAR WILL STOP DEAD ANY TIME THE COOLING SYSTEM FAILS.

This is the number one *mechanical* cause of breakdown. Only flat tires and running out of gas bring more cars to a halt.

IT'S TIME NOW FOR A TRUE CONFESSION:

I, your writer, Barbara, was once driving with my sister and six small children from San Francisco to Lake Tahoe for a vacation. Suddenly, the warning light went on and the car began to lose power so fast that I hardly made it to the side of the road. Steam was rising from under the hood and we—in our ignorance—were all terrified. After being towed to a garage in the nearest town, I was informed that "the head gasket had blown," the engine was ruined, and there was no cure short of an overhaul. What could I do but tell them to go ahead? Between the overhaul and a week's car rental, this misadventure cost me well over $1,000—and that was in the seventies! Imagine what it would cost today.

Today, I know that a blown gasket (head or otherwise) is most unlikely to create such symptoms or ruin an engine. There is a 95% chance that my only trouble was a ruptured hose or fan belt. The next most-likely possibility is that the radiator had sprung a leak.

ANOTHER TRUE CONFESSION:

A year or two later, I was driving the same car on another freeway, going to work, when the overheating warning light went on. I was in a center lane and had to maneuver to the right. The car began to buck and sputter before I was able to stop. I arranged for a tow and was taken to a garage, where I was told that the engine had been ruined and would have to be overhauled—again. Once again, I believed what I was told.

Today, I know this was almost surely another deliberate lie.

Engines are very sturdy. The likelihood of harm occurring in a minute or two is virtually nil.

It is true that if I had kept on forcing the car to drive after the bucking had started, the build-up of heat might have jammed the pistons in the cylinders or even cracked the block. I had not done that, however. Today, under such circumstances, I would arrange for the towing, then would have the cause for the water loss diagnosed before my eyes and then repaired. After having the radiator refilled with coolant, I would try starting the engine—and expect it to function perfectly.

ONE LAST TRUE STORY—THIS TIME FROM VIC:

Early in 1987, I was in the right lane of a freeway in heavy rain and heavy traffic. A big rig was on my tail and just ahead was the very last entrance to the San Francisco Bay Bridge. Suddenly, the overheating light went on and the engine started to falter and lose power rapidly. Fortunately, I was able to pull off to the side after a couple of hundred feet.

Upon examination, I saw that the engine was very hot and water was dripping from under the water pump. I could not examine any further because I was in a business suit and the ground was an inch deep in rainwater. I let the engine cool down for an hour, then slowly filled the radiator with water (which I always carry). The engine started up okay, and I made it home by topping up the radiator three or four times.

The water pump turned out to be leaking. I priced the job at several places, then had it done at a chain for about $170, labor and new pump included.

Had I sent for a tow truck and been taken to a garage, I might have been told the same cock-and-bull story that Barbara believed twice—before she learned better.

The Point of These Stories:

A cooling system is a fail-safe system, designed to prevent damage. Whenever possible, it will signal the driver—or even stop the car—in time to prevent serious harm to the engine.

Knowing this is your best defense against the single costliest kind of automotive rip-off—the false claim by mechanics that a cooling system emergency automatically ruins an engine.

If steam belches from under the hood and/or the engine suddenly halts, this only means that a problem in the cooling system has come on in a sudden, drastic way. The **fan belt** has broken or a **radiator hose** has burst, or the radiator may have been damaged through some trauma. As a result, coolant escapes as steam instead of circulating through the engine.

As we pointed out in chapter 13, The Generating System, fan belts only cost around $5 and can be replaced in fifteen minutes. A radiator hose is even cheaper and quicker to replace. Radiators are expensive; we'll get to them in a moment.

Your overheating warning signal is a direct order to stop and rectify the situation before engine damage can occur. Pull over as quickly as possible. If there is no place to pull off the road, then turn on your emergency signals and stop in the best spot you can. Lift the hood so that more air can get to the engine. (Be careful of any escaping steam.)

Study the situation. See whether a hose or the fan belt has broken or if the car is leaking from underneath. If there are no leaks or breaks, the car probably overheated because of insufficient coolant. Allow the engine to cool for an hour before adding water, since adding cool water too soon causes the metal parts to contract too quickly and may cause damage.

THE COOLING SYSTEM

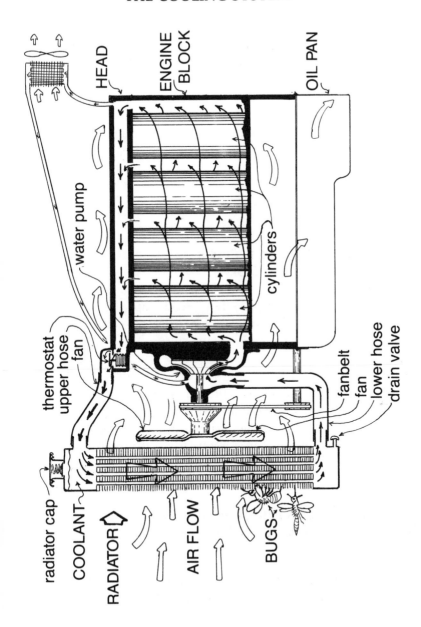

HOW THE COOLING SYSTEM WORKS:

Virtually all recent cars are "water-cooled." When the engine reaches a certain temperature, a **thermostat** opens, allowing a **pump** to start **coolant** circulating between the **engine** and the **radiator,** much the way your heart pumps blood through your system.

The coolant absorbs heat from the engine, then is cooled by the outside air fanned around the radiator, then is pumped back to absorb more heat.

And that's all there is to it.

IT'S A SIMPLE SYSTEM WITH A CONFUSING TERMINOLOGY.

For example, the "cooling system" feeds into the "heating system," but is totally unrelated to the "air-conditioning system."

"Coolant" refers to whatever is in the radiator—usually a 50-50 mixture of water and antifreeze. Antifreeze (propylene glycol) is now used in summer as well as winter, since this amazing chemical both lowers the freezing point *and* raises the boiling point of water. In other words, "anti-freeze" is also "anti-boil," and "anti-rust" as well.

WITH PROPER MAINTENANCE, COOLING SYSTEM BREAKDOWN CAN BE REDUCED TO A MINIMUM.

Winterize ("power flush") every time your coolant is changed. "Winterizing" means draining, flushing, and refilling the whole cooling system, checking the belts, hoses, thermostat, and radiator cap, and doing a pressure test to check for leaks. The job takes about half an hour, plus the cost of the coolant and any parts that need replacing. Expect to pay between $35 and $45 for most models. Flat fees of around $30 are available at chains.

"Winterizing" should be done every two years in mild climates, every fall in moderate climates, and both spring and fall in severe climates, such the northern United States or Canada.

YOUR CAR MAY OVERHEAT EVEN THOUGH NOTHING IS SERIOUSLY WRONG.

At times, when driving in very hot weather, especially in congested traffic, your gauge will indicate that your engine is heating up, or your warning light will start flashing intermittently. Most of the time, this means only that not enough cool air is being fanned in to keep the coolant temperature down.

To prevent your coolant from boiling over, turn off the air conditioner, turn on the heater, and open the windows. In this way, some of the engine heat will be diverted into the car.

If this doesn't work, you'll have to pull over, turn off the motor, lift the hood, and wait an hour.

IF OVERHEATING BECOMES FREQUENT, LOOK FOR THE CAUSE.

A dirty radiator is often responsible. Radiators collect bugs and dirt like crazy. Luckily, they can be rinsed clean in minutes.

The radiator cap is another probability. Let your mechanic show you if it's worn. Should you need a new one, count on spending between $10 and $15, parts and labor included. Or you can save a few dollars by buying a new cap from an auto parts store and putting it on yourself.

Rust forms in radiators, especially if you have been using water only for a coolant, instead of adding antifreeze. Cleaning rust out is called a **flush.** It usually costs around $30, including a gallon of fresh antifreeze. Cut-rate places may charge as little as $20.

The thermostat may be at fault. If stuck, it can prevent circulation of coolant. Figure on half an hour to examine and replace, plus around $10 for the part. Consider your local going rates and apply the FAIR PRICE FORMULA.

The ignition timing can also be checked. If badly adjusted, the timing can cause the engine to overheat. With modern diagnostic equipment, timing can be checked and corrected in a matter of minutes.

Also, make sure that your **fan belt** is not frayed or worn and is properly tight.

If the Above Are All Normal, You Will Have to Spend More For Diagnosis and Repair.

A pressure test costs about $10 and will locate possible leaks in fittings and joints. The cost of fixing leaks depends on where they are located.

Upper and lower radiator hoses should also be examined. If faulty, you can have either replaced in half an hour, both in forty-five or fifty minutes. (When the mechanic is already "in" a system, a second job tends to take less time.)

A small leak in the radiator sometimes can be sealed by an inexpensive additive. It's worth a try. Moderate leaks require the removal, repair, and reinstallation of the radiator. This can run between $60 to over $100, depending on the extent of the damage.

Replacement of a badly damaged or rusted-out radiator takes about an hour, plus $125 to $250 for the new radiator. Check into the price for your own model and use the FAIR PRICE FORMULA.

Water pumps spring leaks when their bearings and or seals give out. Pumps are usually replaced rather than repaired. The job takes up to two hours, while pumps cost from $40 to $100.

If you have air conditioning or power steering, always expect to pay a premium in labor, since their presence makes it harder to get at the car's cooling system.

HOW THE HEATER AND DEFROSTER WORK:

When you turn on the heater or defroster, a fan blows over the **heater core,** which is a little radiator that fills up with hot coolant. The **heater hose** is the part most likely to go wrong. In most cars, it costs $20 to $30 to replace.

If coolant starts dripping onto the carpet on the passenger side, or if the windshield clouds up when you use the defroster, then the heater core may be defective. Repair costs will vary wildly with make and model, from well under $100 to well over $200. Fortunately, heater cores seldom fail.

AIR-COOLED ENGINES:

To cool the engine, air is fanned all over and between the

cylinders and head, which are porcupined with protruding **cooling fins.** Although this method has gone out of style, it still survives in some older Volkswagens, Corvairs, and others.

One problem with air-cooling is that the fins collect dirt and oil and tend to clog, requiring cleaning. Worse yet, the big fan tends to break down, which leads to big expenses. Replacing the fan requires three to five hours, plus the price of a new fan. Renewing the housing is also a three to five-hour job.

TO SUM UP:

COOLING SYSTEMS ARE VERY SIMPLE BUT VERY CRUCIAL.

THEY ARE RESPONSIBLE FOR MORE BREAKDOWNS THAN ANY OTHER KIND OF MECHANICAL FAILURE.

THE MOST COMMON TROUBLES ARE EASILY IDENTIFIED AND CHEAP TO FIX.

HOWEVER, THE CAUSES OF CHRONIC OVERHEATING CAN BE TRICKY TO DIAGNOSE, AND SOME LESS-COMMON REPAIRS ARE COSTLY.

WHEN THE CAR OVERHEATS, STOP AS SOON AS POSSIBLE AND WAIT FOR THE ENGINE TO COOL. THIS WILL PREVENT ENGINE DAMAGE.

BEWARE OF MECHANICS WHO PASS OFF COOLING SYS-TEM EMERGENCIES AS RUINED ENGINES.

USE THE *FAIR PRICE FORMULA* FOR COOLING-SYSTEM REPAIRS.

16

The Lubrication System

THE LUBRICATION SYSTEM PUMPS OIL THROUGH THE ENGINE, REDUCING FRICTION BY COATING THE MOVING METAL PARTS.

Oil is stored in an **oil pan** underneath the engine. When you start your car, the **oil pump** draws the oil up through the **oil pickup screen,** passes it through the pump, then pressure drives it through the **oil filter.** From there, the oil goes upward through the **ducts** to lubricate the various moving parts of the engine. After being squirted all around these parts, the oil drips back down into the pan again.

OIL STARVATION AND *DIRT* ARE THE GREAT ENEMIES OF YOUR ENGINE.

Lubrication is a life-and-death matter. Without a coating of

THE LUBRICATING SYSTEM

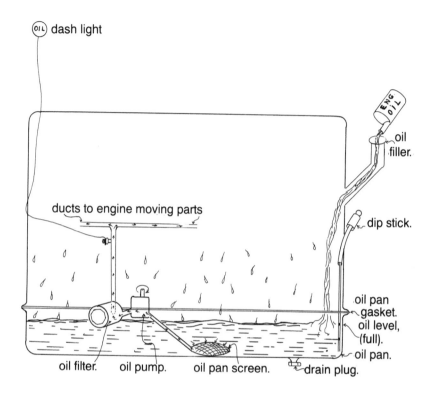

clean oil, the moving parts are quickly damaged by heat and wear. An engine run without any oil is destroyed immediately. An engine run on too little oil or dirty oil is destroyed gradually and inevitably.

Always *warm up* your car well before driving. Warming up pumps the oil through the engine, coating the parts before they have to move. After a minute or so, you can begin to drive at reasonable speed to allow the engine to continue warming. Don't tear off impatiently like some TV detective or you will pay for it in engine repairs.

A REGULAR *OIL CHANGE, FILTER CHANGE,* AND *"LUBE" JOB* IS THE BEST PREVENTIVE MAINTENANCE:

The oil filter is the guardian of the system. If clogged, however, it gives out no distress signal but instead sends the dirty oil through a bypass. The dirt then collects and begins to erode the engine.

Change the filter each time you change the oil. This should be done according to the schedule in your owner's manual. If you don't have a manual, play it safe and change every 3,000 miles or whenever the oil starts to look dirty, whichever comes sooner.

Oil level is also crucial. Check it every time you refuel. Always keep it above the *add* line but just a little below the *full*.

Oil composition codes guide you to the right oil. Oils for trucks, gasoline cars, and diesels all differ in composition and are coded accordingly. Every can of oil has a code number stamped on top. If you drive a car fueled by gasoline, only use oil coded API-SE, API-SF or API-SG. If you have a diesel, only use API-CD.

The weight of oil also affects function. Light weight oils, such as 10W or 20W, confer certain benefits and heavier weight oils, such as 30W or 40W, offer others. Unless your owner's manual specifies otherwise, use a "multiviscosity" 10W–30W or 10W–40W, which combines the advantages of all grades. Whenever you add oil make sure it is of the same weight as you have been using. If a change of season or climate requires a different weight, start fresh with a change of oil.

A "lube" (or "grease job") should be included in with the

oil-and-filter change. This consists of pumping lubricant into the **grease nipples** located at all moving joints of the car, such as the steering, the tail-shaft, the wheels, and so forth.

The cost of an oil, filter, and lube job depends on where you get it done. Most service sources charge between $20 and $40, all inclusive. Flat-fee specialists offer the job for around $16 to $20. Since this is a very simple job there's no reason to pay a premium price.

LUBRICATING SYSTEMS ARE SUBJECT TO ONLY A FEW OTHER PROBLEMS:

Oil pickup screens may become blocked if oil is allowed to become extremely filthy. With proper maintenance, this problem is totally avoidable.

Oil pans sometimes spring gasket leaks.

Oil pumps can wear out, but rarely do.

Costs will vary for these problems. In some models, parts are quite accessible and can be replaced in an hour or two. In others, the engine has to be lifted to get at them, which adds greatly to the cost. You'll need to use your communication skills (and perhaps consult a dealer) to find out what procedures are needed for your car. Then use the FAIR PRICE FORMULA.

TO SUM UP:

ALWAYS MAKE SURE YOUR CAR HAS ENOUGH OF THE RIGHT KIND OF OIL AND THAT IT'S CLEAN.

CHANGE YOUR OIL AND OIL FILTER REGULARLY.

WARM UP BEFORE YOU DRIVE.

17

The Exhaust System

THE EXHAUST SYSTEM GETS RID OF THE BURNED FUEL (WASTE PRODUCTS) LEFT OVER FROM THE PROCESS OF COMBUSTION.

It cools, cleans, quiets, and vents these poisonous—*very poisonous*—substances.

EXHAUST PROBLEMS ARE FAIRLY COMMON AND NOT HARD TO DIAGNOSE.

They tend to **make noise** and **smell bad.** Often there's a shotgun racket called **backfiring.** Let your mechanic trace the exact source. Since exhaust problems spell danger, have such repairs attended to at once.

Service sources specializing in exhaust system repairs are

called **muffler shops.** Check them out for the best combination of low price and strong warranty.

HOW THE EXHAUST SYSTEM WORKS:

Waste gases are collected into an **exhaust manifold** that connects to an **exhaust pipe.** Before being expelled, these wastes pass through a **catalytic converter** (to reduce pollution), a **muffler** (to reduce noise), a **resonator** (to reduce noise further), and finally go out the **tail pipe** to the open air.

The Exhaust Manifold:

This part gathers exhaust gases from each combustion chamber through **exhaust ports,** sometimes aided by **air injectors,** which contribute to the more efficient burning of the fuel-air mixture. The **exhaust manifold gasket** forms a seal between the manifold and the engine.

Four- and six-cylinder cars have a single exhaust manifold. Eights have two.

Replacement of an exhaust manifold gasket is one of those jobs that can vary dramatically in cost, depending on its accessibility in different models. Some take one hour, while others take as much as four. Fortunately, exhaust manifold gaskets don't blow very often. However, if it should happen to you, and you get a high labor estimate, look up the time figure in the *Chilton Guide.*

At the connection of the exhaust manifold with the exhaust pipe is a second, smaller **gasket.** This sometimes springs a leak. Although this gasket costs around $5, the labor may take from one to several hours, depending on make and model. Investigate, and use your FAIR PRICE FORMULA.

The Catalytic Converter:

This is a widely used antipollution device that neutralizes most of the byproducts produced by combustion—chemicals such as hydrocarbons, oxides of nitrogen, and carbon monoxide. We don't mean to panic you, but these byproducts are deadly poisons.

Catalytic converters use "catalysts" to convert these poisons into harmless substances, such as water, carbon dioxide, and elemental nitrogen and oxygen.

If your car requires unleaded fuel only, it probably has a converter; recent registration laws require them (or comparable devices). The test for the efficiency of a car's antipollution system is called an **emission control test** (**smog test**) and usually costs between $15 and $30.

Theoretically, catalytic converters should outlast your car, but because they are sensitive to engine problems, chronically dirty or dysfunctional engines can destroy catalytic converters, as can the lead in regular gas. So if your car has a catalytic converter, change your oil and filter extra frequently, and *use unleaded fuel only.*

Replacement of a catalytic converter runs between $200 and $600—Chryslers costing the least and full-sized Fords the most.

The Muffler:

This part literally "muffles" the noise of combustion in the engine. Because it takes a lot of abuse, it tends to wear out. Replacing a muffler takes from one to two hours, plus the price of the replacement. Comparison-shop muffler specialists and expect to pay a total of between $70 to $100. *Heavy duty stainless steel* mufflers and tail pipes are more costly but will last the life of the car.

The Tail Pipe and Resonator:

These parts take about half an hour to replace, plus the cost of the parts, which run to about $20 each. Check the prices for your own make and model. Flat-fee places will probably save you about 35%, and are recommended.

Combination Jobs:

Mechanics often recommend replacing two or three exhaust parts—such as the muffler, tail pipe, and resonator—at the same time. This is usually a good idea. All these parts are very exposed to the elements and tend to corrode and rust together. It costs more to separate them than to remove and replace the whole section. Also, combinations save time that would be wasted hunting around for the exact source of a leak.

TO SUM UP:

THE EXHAUST SYSTEM COOLS, CLEANS, QUIETS, AND VENTS WASTE PRODUCTS FROM COMBUSTION.

THESE WASTES ARE EXTREMELY HAZARDOUS, SO DON'T DELAY REPAIRS.

EXHAUST PROBLEMS CREATE SUCH A RACKET AND/OR STINK THAT YOU'LL KNOW WHEN THEY HAPPEN.

COMPARISON-SHOP THE MUFFLER SPECIALISTS FOR THE BEST REPAIR DEALS.

18

The Suspension System (Including Tires)

THE SUSPENSION SYSTEM PROVIDES CUSHIONING BETWEEN THE WHEELS AND THE CAR BODY TO REDUCE WEAR AND SMOOTH OUT THE RIDE.

A car and its passengers need to be cushioned from the rough surface of the road. To do this, **springs** are placed between the wheels and the car body to absorb the bumps.

But springs bounce—and bounce and bounce. This bounce must be absorbed. Traditionally, cars used **shock absorbers** to control this bouncing. Most recent models use **Mac-Pherson struts** for front suspension. MacPhersons combine spring, shocks, and other parts in a single unit, both improving and simplifying the system. Unfortunately, they are difficult to remove and therefore expensive to repair or replace.

WHY CARS COME WITH SUSPENSION SYSTEMS

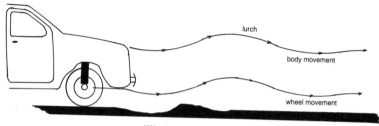

Without a suspension system

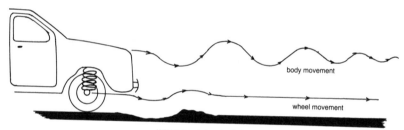

With springs, but no shock absorbers

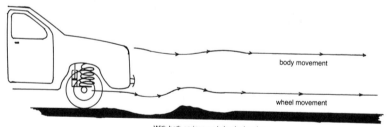

With both springs and shock absorbers

Most other suspension parts are there to serve and support the springs and shocks or to allow you to change and correct course smoothly. There are more "arms" and "knuckles" and "joints," and "bearings," etc., than we could name or you could keep straight. And no two systems are quite the same.

Our illustrations show how typical systems might work on a front wheel and a pair of rear ones.

FORTUNATELY, SUSPENSION SYSTEM CARE IS LARGELY A MATTER OF MAINTENANCE.

Lubrication:

Suspension systems must be kept lubricated, or "greased" to prevent friction wear. As we mentioned in chapter 16, The Lubrication System, every oil-and-filter change should include a "lube" job. In severe climates, this should be done twice a year.

"Packing" of the front wheel bearings of rear-wheel drive cars is usually done every spring. This is a cleaning as well as lubricating job. It takes an hour and is usually combined with other jobs in progress, such as removing snow tires. In front-wheel drive cars, the rear wheel bearings will have to be repacked on the same regular basis.

Frequent and consistent lubrication will help to prevent suspension system problems. Your annual diagnostic checkup may also forewarn you if any are upcoming.

SUSPENSION SYSTEM PROBLEMS:

Rough road bounce, often combined with steering problems and uneven tire wear, indicates worn shock absorbers.

THE SUSPENSION SYSTEM, REAR

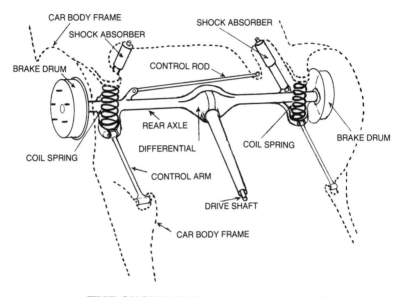

THE SUSPENSION SYSTEM, FRONT

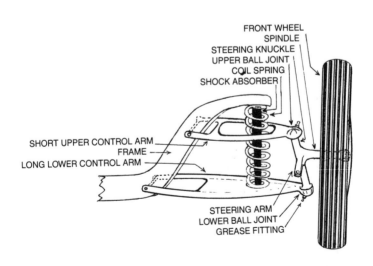

To test for worn shocks, just push down suddenly and hard on a fender. If that section of the car starts bouncing around, your shocks have had it and should be replaced. If the section goes down but comes back to rest with little or no bounce, the shocks are okay.

A pair of **rear shock absorbers** average around $75 to replace, plus or minus $20, for all cars. Costs vary wildly for **front shocks,** from around $65 a pair to twice that much, depending on the design of your car. **Replacing MacPherson struts** can cost up to twice as much.

If power steering is sloppy or allows too much free play, suspect worn ball joints. On most cars, a pair of **upper or lower ball joints** cost between $50 and $75 each pair to replace. Some Fords may cost a good deal more.

The rear axle bearing seal tends to spring leaks. A new seal, installed, averages around $30, with Fords and many imports costing below average and Chryslers a bit above.

NOISES HEARD WHILE DRIVING:

A grinding noise coming from a front wheel while you are driving suggests problems with the front wheel bearings. Bearing problems can be *very dangerous,* as the wheel may tend to lock or brake unexpectedly. *Stop at once* and send for a tow service. **Replacement of the front bearing** should total between $40 and $50, with Chrysler cars somewhat higher.

A loud bang when you put the car into gear may mean a worn universal. You can tell by the source of the sound, which will be coming from the rear. **Replacement of a Universal** will average around $50.

A grinding noise from a rear wheel is probably caused by an axle bearing. This also is *very dangerous*. Again, *stop!* **Replacing the axle bearing** should cost between $50 and $80.

A whine that comes from the rear during driving is probably caused by a worn differential. The **differential** is the connection between the transmission and the rear wheels that drives the rear axles and allows for different wheel speeds during turns. When the differential goes, you can assume that a lot of other parts have gone or will soon go and that an overhaul is necessary.

If you have a front wheel drive car, and you notice a "knicking and knacking" clatter at low speeds, you may be having trouble with one or both of the constant velocity (CV) joints on your front wheels. This is an expensive proposition which varies by make or model. Have your mechanic explain his estimate.

The entire system should be put through a diagnostic test. All exterior parts supporting the system (such as seals, gaskets, etc.) should be replaced, along with worn interior parts.

Overhaul of the differential and its related parts is a big job, taking a full working day and calling for the replacement of a variable number of parts. Expect a total of between $350 and $450—less in rural areas and for most imports. Fortunately, this is not a job that happens frequently.

If you are given estimates that are well out of line with our figures, use your FAIR PRICE FORMULA. Have your mechanic put his estimated time in writing and check it against *Chilton.* Have him also list in writing the parts that he intends to replace, then research their prices.

TIRES:

Tires take, and must soften, the immediate impact of the road. For this reason, they wear fast and also greatly affect the feel of the ride.

Many different types of tires are available. **Belted ply** are better than **bias ply,** and **radials** are best of all. **All-season tires** outlast traditional **snow tires** and can be used year-round. Retreads can save up to half in price, but don't buy any rated less than A or B by the NTDRA (National Tire Dealers and Retreaders Association). Your dealer can tell you the rating.

Always use the same kind of tire on all four wheels, and whatever kind you use, buy them from a tire store such as Goodyear, or a department store chain such as Sears. New car dealers or service stations will tend to charge more.

Tire Maintenance:

Tires should be inflated according to the manufacturer's recommendations—usually printed on the side of the tires. They should also be rotated about every 5,000 miles. The wheels should be balanced and the alignment checked at the same time. Tires of the same construction—such as either bias ply or radials—should be used on all four wheels. To neglect these rules will cost you greatly in tire wear.

Proper inflation keeps the tires from wearing unevenly. Check the look of your tires. If the outer rims seem to be wearing faster, your tires are underinflated. If the center strips are wearing faster, your tires are overinflated. Have your mechanic add or let out air. (It should cost nothing.) Tire wear in patches or at odd "feathery" angles is due to a problem with rotation, balancing, or alignment.

Rotation consists of switching the positions of all four tires to achieve even wear. It takes under half an hour and costs an average of $15.

Balancing means attaching little weights to the wheels to compensate for irregularities in the manufacture of the tires. It takes about half an hour and costs about $18. Any time you have a front tire fixed or replaced, have the wheel balance checked and corrected. There should be no additional charge.

Alignment means setting the wheels at the correct angles to straighten themselves out when in motion. (There are several such angles, but the one you are most likely to hear mentioned is the "toe-in.") Poor alignment will wear out tires faster than any other cause.

Checking alignment takes minimum time. **Correcting alignment** takes from a few minutes to an hour, depending on the car. It can cost between $25 and $60. Cut-rate chains will do the check *and* the alignment for a flat fee of around $20.

Tire Problems:

If the car pulls to the left or right, or if the front end vibrates at high speed, check first for a low or flat tire. Then, if everything looks fine, have the tires checked for balance.

If the car still pulls to the side or vibrates, have the "spindle" nuts checked. They should be locked with a pin in a slightly loosened position—a simple, minimum-price job.

If the steering wheel shakes at any speed, the front wheels are probably unbalanced. Unevenly worn tires will confirm the diagnosis.

If a tire has a slow puncture leak, it will have to be removed, patched, and reinstalled. This is an easy job; go for a second opinion if someone says you need a new tire. Repair should cost under $10.

Properly Inflated, Rotated, Balanced, and Aligned Tires Will Wear Together and Can Be Replaced Together.

In respect to both ride and long-term economy, replacing all four tires at once is the ideal. Tires of the same make, tread, and age wear far more slowly. However, if you must buy a single tire, replace it with the same tread and structure as the tires on the other wheels.

TO SUM UP:

THE SUSPENSION SUPPORTS THE WEIGHT OF THE CAR, FORMING A BUFFER BETWEEN THE ROUGHNESS OF THE ROAD AND THE CAR AND ITS PASSENGERS.

IT CONSISTS OF SPRINGS, SHOCKS (OR STRUTS), AND THEIR SUPPORT SYSTEM.

ABOVE ALL, THE SUSPENSION SYSTEM NEEDS REGULAR MAINTENANCE.

TO EXTEND TIRE LIFE, KEEP THEM PROPERLY INFLATED, BALANCED AND ALIGNED, AND ROTATE THEM TWICE A YEAR.

19

The Air-Conditioning System

THE AIR CONDITIONING SYSTEM KEEPS PASSENGERS COOL IN HOT WEATHER.

Once thought of as a luxury, many now consider it a necessity—at luxury prices.

THE SYSTEM ITSELF IS SIMPLE, YET REQUIRES DELICATE HANDLING:

Refrigerant (usually **Freon**) is circulated around a closed system. An **evaporator** (under the dash) absorbs heat from within the passenger compartment, turning the Freon into a gas. The **compressor** puts the Freon under pressure, then passes it to the **condensor,** where the heat is absorbed by the air, cooling the Freon to a liquid again, then pumping it back to the **evaporator.**

This cycle repeats continuously, so long as the air conditioner is on.

THREE SIMPLE STEPS WILL HELP MAINTAIN THE SYSTEM AND PREVENT TROUBLE:

First, keep the Freon level up to full, and check it periodically.

Second, run the system at least ten minutes weekly, even in winter. This will keep the parts lubricated. Otherwise, the system may dry out and shrink, causing Freon leaks and damage to parts.

Third, have the system serviced every spring—and every fall as well in climates where you use the system all year around. Lack of proper servicing creates the same problems as failing to give the system its weekly run.

Servicing entails cleaning the condensor surface, adjusting the compressor belt, flushing and refilling the system with Freon, examining for leaks, and testing. You can expect to pay between $50 and $65—even more for some elite models.

YOU KNOW SOMETHING IS WRONG IF LITTLE OR NO COOL AIR BLOWS IN.

Repair costs can range from unreasonable to sickeningly unreasonable.

The compressor belt drives the compressor. If too loose, it can be adjusted in minutes. If worn out, it can be replaced for an average of $25.

Replacement of the compressor will run from $250 to over $500, with GMs tending to be the *most* unreasonable.

The expansion valve (connected to the evaporator) regulates the circulation of the Freon. If clogged, stuck, or damaged, it keeps the car from cooling. Replacement costs between $100 and $170. In this case, GMs are the *least* unreasonable.

Freon circulates through hoses, which can cost between $75 and $150 (or even more!) to replace.

Replacing the blower motor, at least, is not too exorbitant, because it is the same motor that is used in the heating system. With a few exceptions, a new one runs between $70 and $100 installed.

We don't claim such prices are fair—But they happen to be the going rates. Automotive air-conditioning mechanics have a virtual monopoly, since few but experts will touch this tricky system. Also, air conditioning is still considered a luxury, so the specialists charge luxury prices.

TO SUM UP:

TO PREVENT DAMAGE TO YOUR AIR CONDITIONING SYSTEM:

KEEP UP THE FREON LEVEL
RUN THE SYSTEM WEEKLY
SERVICE ANNUALLY

IF YOU NEED REPAIRS ANYWAY, PREPARE TO EMPTY YOUR WALLET.

20

Dealing with Dealers, New Cars, High Tech, and Warranties

DON'T SKIP THIS CHAPTER, EVEN IF YOU DIDN'T BUY YOUR CAR NEW.

Dealerships, new cars, warranties, and high tech all belong under one heading because new cars come with warranties that require them to be serviced at dealerships. Some warranties extend to five or seven years, so quite a few older cars are still partially covered.

Besides, as cars get more and more high tech, we're all going to become more dependent on dealership service. The more high-tech equipment in your car, the more dependent you will be.

DEALERSHIPS:

The first thing to realize is that dealers are not employees of car manufacturers. Dealerships are franchises and dealers are independent business people who buy from manufacturers to resell to the public. As part of the deal, they also contract to provide the service guaranteed by the manufacturer's warranty.

Dealership mechanics aren't always employees of the dealers either. Sometimes they (or their bosses) are subcontracted by a dealer to run that aspect of the business.

So, if a new car is defective or a service job is badly done, manufacturers, dealers, and mechanics are in a great position to pass the buck back and forth to each other—the buck being you.

WARRANTIES:

The next thing to realize is that warranties are meant to protect manufacturers first, dealers second, and the car owner last.

If it were not for these warranties, the same laws would govern cars as any other products. That is, if you were sold a lemon, you could take it back for a refund or exchange.

This is harder to do with a car. But times are changing, and you can get help if you're willing to fight for it.

Warranties and Consumer Protection:

Thanks to the consumer protection movement, warranties are improving steadily and dealers are living up to them better. Where they do not, consumers can turn for help to the Better Business Bureau, as well as to the manufacturer and many Federal, state and private agencies.

In the *Appendix: Helpful Lists & Addresses,* you will find the information needed to contact such agencies. But always begin by contacting your manufacturer's owner relations department first. The address and phone number will be in your owner's manual.

Warranties and Maintenance:

Warranties are full of pitfalls. Different systems are covered for different lengths of time. To keep the coverage on the parts still under warranty, you may need to have the *entire* car serviced by the dealer. Also, if you fail to keep up recommended maintenance schedules, you may lose your entire coverage.

Sometimes you may have work done at any of the manufacturer's dealerships, and sometimes only at the dealership where you bought the car. Sometimes dealerships can refuse to do warranty service on any car they have not sold.

Warranties are also "limited." They cover certain problems and not others. Coverage differs from make to make, so any time you are considering buying a new car, study its warranty. *First.*

Warranties and Repairs:

Dealers make little profit on repairs done under warranty. Reimbursement comes from the manufacturer—at a rate that favors the manufacturer. Naturally, dealership shops make up the "loss" as best they can—mainly by overcharging customers for jobs not covered by the warranty—sometimes jobs that don't need doing in the first place.

Warranties are tricky. Usually, only problems due to "defects in manufacture" are covered. In other words, if they can find a way to blame the problem on you and not the car, they will.

A warranty can end up costing a driver more than it saves. For this reason, many warranties are abandoned before they ever run out.

Yet This Crazy System Can Actually Work to Your Advantage:

First, it forces you to keep your car well maintained—and consistent maintenance prevents at least 80% of potential automobile repairs. Forced maintenance benefits everyone. Your car stays in better condition longer, and the dealership is not stuck with doing a lot of repairs that could have been prevented.

Second, you tend to get skilled service. Dealerships usually service just one or two makes. They have replacement parts on hand. They are required to send their mechanics to seminars and training sessions.

Third, you can make the most of your warranty, while it's still in force. Every time you go in for mandatory service, bring a written list of every little thing that's wrong and under warranty, and have it fixed. This way, you can get and keep your car in the best possible working order.

Remember that all dealerships are not the same. If your

warranty permits, compare the local dealerships servicing your make and choose the best.

DEALERSHIPS AND HIGH TECH:

According to *High Technology Magazine,* the world's biggest consumer of computer chips is *General Motors.* This tiny fact speaks volumes.

Since 1977, silicon chips have taken over many automotive functions. By the end of the century, many of us will be driving vehicles in which central computers run almost everything.

In other words, the "car" is being reinvented. The knowledge acquired by the best mechanics of ten years ago is already obsolete. Backyard tinkering may soon be a thing of the past.

Many repairs are going to be easier—a matter of replacing chips. Whether we will pay more or less for this will depend on decisions within the industry. Recently, Mitsubishi took the lead by giving a three-year/36,000 mile warranty on virtually all high-tech components. These components include an electronically controlled air conditioner, alternator, automatic transmission, cruise control, power steering, and suspension. This warranty shows a lot of confidence in the durability of these components. If other carmakers fall into line, we may all end up with lower repair bills down the road.

For the present, every manufacturer is still experimenting with its own, new high-tech systems. As a result, we will all become more dependent on dealership service than ever before.

TO SUM UP:

TO KEEP YOUR WARRANTY, YOU HAVE TO PATRONIZE YOUR DEALERSHIP REPAIR SHOP AND KEEP UP THE MANUFACTURER'S RECOMMENDED MAINTENANCE SCHEDULES.

THIS HAS THE ADVANTAGE OF GETTING YOUR CAR THE BEST CARE.

UNFORTUNATELY, WHERE THEY CAN CHARGE, MOST TEND TO CHARGE HIGH.

THE MORE HIGH TECH YOUR CAR, THE MORE DEPENDENT YOU BECOME ON DEALERSHIP SERVICE.

AS THE WHOLE INDUSTRY GOES MORE HIGH TECH, THE MORE DEPENDENT WE'RE ALL GOING TO BE.

ALL THINGS CONSIDERED, WE WOULD RECOMMEND AGAINST BUYING EXTENDED WARRANTIES OR SERVICE CONTRACTS.

21

Thinking of Your Mechanic as Almost Human

BACK IN CHAPTER 2, ABOUT THE FOUR PLACES TO GET WORK DONE—

We probably gave you the impression that you would be spending the rest of your days hopping from mechanic to mechanic and specialist to specialist, always looking for the cheapest job.

Actually, we wouldn't want you to do that. You don't go to the cheapest place to get your hair cut. You go to the best you can find within the limits of your budget.

It's the same with your car. But if we left you with that first impression, it was for a very good reason.

WE WERE TRYING TO SHOW YOU THAT YOU HAVE OPTIONS—AND *RIGHTS*:

- The right to ask questions.
- The right to shop around.
- The right to second and third opinions.
- The right to say no.
- The right not to be bullied.
- The right not to be fleeced.
- The right to consider your own needs.
- The right to find a good mechanic.

THE QUALITIES OF A GOOD MECHANIC:

In chapter 2, we introduced you to a list of traits belonging to the good mechanic. This is a good place to summarize and amplify those traits for you.

The good mechanic is open to communication. He listens with respect to your opinions, answers your questions willingly and clearly, and works cooperatively with you to arrive at the best solution to a problem.

He is competent. He fixes what's wrong, usually on the first try. He fixes it right, with no bolts coming loose the next week.

He is reliable. If he says your car will be ready at a certain time, it will be. If there is an unavoidable delay, he contacts you. If he promises to phone at a certain time, he does. His final bills are in line with his estimates.

He is competitive in pricing policy. He may not offer the cheapest deal around, but he will deliver *the most quality for the money.*

Above all, he is *honest*—**in every sense of the word.** He does not give snap diagnoses before he is sure what is wrong. He does not try to cover up his own ignorance or take advantage of yours. He does not give estimate prices that turn out to cover only a fraction of the actual costs. He is glad to put things in writing and to stick to his agreements.

YOU CAN NEVER PREDICT WHERE SUCH A MECHANIC WILL BE FOUND.

He may run his own independent shop, or be a partner or employee almost anywhere. He may work for a dealer, and possibly even for a chain. He may work in your own neighborhood, or across town. The only way you're going to find him is to be out there, looking.

Ideally, he will be an all-around mechanic, who networks with specialists, just as doctors and dentists do.

ONCE YOU'VE FOUND HIM, HOW SHOULD YOU TREAT HIM?

With helpfulness. Come prepared to work cooperatively with him. Have your car's symptoms clearly described, preferably on paper. Don't diagnose, but do make intelligent suggestions. List the symptoms accurately, then add, for example, "I was thinking it may be the fuel pump."

With clear intentions. Decide in advance what is the purpose of each visit, whether it's to fix one thing or several. Don't have him work up his estimate, then suddenly start recollecting other things for him to look into or do.

With professional courtesy. Make appointments, then show up on time. Be polite, gracious, and appreciative of his abilities. Thank him for work well done and for meeting deadlines.

With friendliness, but not with friendship. Don't date him or join the same bowling team. You would not want to risk losing your mechanic over some personal quarrel.

With firmness. Show that you expect and won't settle for less than a continued high level of service.

With guarded loyalty. Continue to patronize him, but only as long as it continues to be in your own best interest. Allow him to do certain jobs that you might get done more cheaply elsewhere, just to affirm your trust and to get continuity of care. If his work deteriorates, point it out and allow him another chance. But not more than one.

With a touch of skepticism. When in doubt, go elsewhere for a second opinion—just as you would if he were a doctor.

Be Understanding, But Not *Too* Understanding:

Your mechanic may have a boss to please or regulations to meet. If he's working for himself, he has bills to pay. He may have private worries, or too much work on his hands—or too little. None of this excuses incompetent, careless work.

DON'T FORGET TO PROTECT YOURSELF:

Use the FAIR PRICE FORMULA to judge the fairness of both estimates and final bills. Match every final bill against the estimate. Have the mechanic explain any discrepancies. Examine the work done and any replaced parts. Always test drive your car before paying. Save all your itemized receipts.

BE AWARE OF *MECHANIC'S LIENS*:

The law usually requires that you pay a mechanic what he claims is owed. Otherwise, he can hold your car—or even sell it. This right is called a *mechanic's lien.* Your best preventive is a written estimate—made out on a work-order form—complete with the mechanic's signature.

Never sign an estimate or work order that is not completely filled out. If there are blank spaces, put a line through them. Think of a blank space as the equivalent of a blank check.

IF YOU ARE NOT SATISFIED WITH A JOB, OR IF YOU FEEL YOU'VE BEEN OVERCHARGED, OR IF PROBLEMS ARISE LATER:

- Complain as quickly as possible.
- Try to work things out through friendly discussion.
- Take your complaint to the boss.
- If your complaint isn't resolved, don't be intimidated.
- Persist.

IF WORSE COMES TO WORSE:

Take your case to your automobile club, the Better Business Bureau, or even Small Claims Court. No lawyers are allowed into Small Claims Court and fees are only a few dollars. Both sides state their case and show their evidence. You may be awarded up to $1,500—depending on the limits in your particular state.

AND IF VERY WORSE COMES TO VERY WORST:

You may lose out. This isn't a perfectly just world.

BECAUSE THEY'RE HUMAN, SOME MECHANICS ARE IN INCOMPETENT AND OTHERS ARE DISHONEST.

The most likely place to meet incompetent ones is at big chains, where the pay is relatively low. That's why it's best to rely on chains for basic jobs only. It takes quite a different level of skills to change your oil or to put on new tires or even to reline your brakes, than to diagnose a tricky problem in a combustion chamber.

The most likely place to meet dishonest ones is on the road, especially in service stations on or near freeways where they never expect to see their customers again. That's where you'll hear that your vapor lock is a rusted-out radiator or a burned-out engine. That's where they'll let the air out of your tires, then say that you need new ones—or actually wreck an engine part.

The best defense against trickery is knowledge and watchfulness. Always get out of your car when it is being serviced at a strange station. Watch everything that is done. Have the attendant check the tires and under the hood before your eyes. Don't leave for the bathroom or the snack bar until the work is done and you have pulled away from the service area and parked. Even if you have been towed in, don't agree to leave the car for any repair that sounds fishy to you. It's better to pay for a second tow than to pay for an overhaul you don't need.

TO SUM UP:

A GOOD MECHANIC IS COMMUNICATIVE, COMPETENT, RELIABLE, HONEST—AND HARD TO FIND.

KEEP ON LOOKING.

WHEN YOU FIND HIM, BE RESPECTFUL, GRATEFUL, HELP-FUL, AND UNDERSTANDING—BUT NOT TOO UNDER-STANDING.

BE AWARE OF THE LEGALITIES—*MECHANIC'S LIENS* AND *SMALL CLAIMS COURT.*

ULTIMATELY, IT'S YOUR RESPONSIBILITY TO PROTECT YOURSELF.

SO KEEP ON LEARNING.

22

Pulling It All Together

AS A SORT OF HAIL AND FAREWELL, LET'S SUMMARIZE:

Now you know that there are many different kinds of mechanics, that whichever one is best depends on circumstances, and that it's up to you to determine those circumstances.

The independent diagnostic clinic is the best place to get your car its annual checkup. They've got the equipment and no motivation to be anything but honest.

Combination diagnostic-and-repair clinics are a poor second best, because they've got a vested interest in finding jobs to be done. They should be used where independent diagnostic clinics are not available.

Mass volume specialists, such as muffler shops, offer low prices, usually combined with good service and strong guarantees. They may also try to sell you a bigger job than you need.

Luxury option specialists such as air-conditioning shops, charge high prices for jobs that you may not be able to get done elsewhere, except at a dealership.

National automotive chains and department stores are in the business of selling parts. They will install and service what they sell, charging you well-below-average prices for many basic maintenance and repair jobs. Don't bring them complex diagnostic work, however. And do expect them to try to sell you more than you need.

Dealership shops specialize in your make. The newer or more high-tech your car, the more dependent on their equipment and service you will be. In their favor is expertise. Against is their tendency to overcharge whenever possible to make up for low manufacturer reimbursements on jobs under warranty.

Your good, old-fashioned, all-around mechanic is an endangered species. But it's just possible that you may find a survivor somewhere who is both competent and honest. If you do, give him the lion's share of your business. If you're a steady customer (in an age where steady customers are also an endangered species), he should cherish you too.

BEFORE REPAIRS COME UP, SHOP AROUND FOR THE BEST PLACES TO GET YOUR MAINTENANCE JOBS DONE.

Look at it as a learning experience—a chance to discover your way among the variety of services that are out there, as well as to master the Fair Price Formula and gain in confidence. *Expect* to be treated shabbily in some places and much better in others. Learn to recognize the difference.

FINDING A MECHANIC IS LIKE FINDING A MATE.

Don't expect to meet the right one on the first try. Even if your goal is to settle down forever, realize that the search can take time.

But what do you do, while looking for Mr. Right? And what if you never find him? For one thing, you can learn to enjoy playing the field. That is, you can learn to make the best of all the alternatives available.

In other words, whether you find one all-purpose mechanic you can be true to, or decide you'd rather make the most of the specialists and discounts, you can be happy either way— so long as you're coming from awareness and not ignorance or desperation.

AND SO LONG AS YOU REMEMBER TO APPLY YOUR *FAIR PRICE FORMULA* **AND THE** *TEN STEPS TO HONEST SERVICE*

80% TO 90% OF ALL LEGITIMATE CAR REPAIRS ARE DUE TO NEGLIGENCE!

This means that 80% to 90% of all legitimate car repairs can be prevented. Which also means that by avoiding car abuse and keeping up good maintenance, you can save 80% to 90% on legitimate repair costs.

AT LEAST 50% OF ALL CAR REPAIRS ARE NOT FULLY LEGITIMATE!

This means that knowing your car, having annual diagnostic checkups, going for second opinions, and watching like a hawk when you go in for service on the road, can save you a good half on repairs.

ALL THAT COULD ADD UP TO A HEFTY MONETARY SAVING—

Not to consider your temper and nerves.

TO SUM UP:

WE HOPE THIS BOOK WAS AS ENJOYABLE AND ENLIGHT-ENING TO READ AS IT WAS TO WRITE, AND THAT YOU'LL USE IT FOR A LONG TIME TO COME.

MAY WE WISH YOU A HAPPY, SAFE, CONFIDENT, AND *AFFORDABLE* DRIVING LIFE.

Appendix A

Maintenance

WE'VE PREPARED TWO MAINTENANCE LISTS —ONE ALPHABETICAL, ONE SEASONAL.

Use whichever you prefer. However, since cars vary, also check your owner's manual for exact recommendations for your own model.

Alphabetical Maintenance List

AIR CONDITIONING
Run 10 minutes weekly, all seasons. Service every spring, or twice yearly in climates where system is used year around.

AUTOMATIC TRANSMISSION
Check fluid level whenever oil is changed (every three to six months). Add more when needed.

AIR FILTER
Check whenever oil is changed (every three to six months). Replace if needed.

BATTERY AND ACCESSORIES
Monthly check of fan belt, terminals, cables, and battery water level (if battery is not sealed).

BODY PAINT AND TRIM
Wash at least monthly; polish or wax at least twice a year—more often if you live in a region with severe weather conditions.

BRAKES
Check whenever oil is changed (every three to six months). Replace brake fluid every one to two years. Replace linings when about two-thirds worn.

CATALYTIC CONVERTER (OR OTHER EMISSION CONTROL)
Check at each ignition system checkup (every 5,000 miles, or spring and fall).

CHASSIS LUBRICATION
Have done at every oil change (three to six months). Do more often if road conditions are unusually salty, dusty, or sandy. Have check done for possible leaks from any system.

COOLING SYSTEM

Check belts, hoses, coolant level at every oil change (three to six months). Replace coolant every one to two years, depending on use.

CRANKCASE VENTILATOR VALVE

Check at each oil change (three to six months). Change as needed.

FRONT END ALIGNMENT

Have done every spring and fall, or more often under rough road and bad driving conditions.

FUEL FILTER

Check, preferably replace, spring and fall.

IGNITION SYSTEM (INCLUDING SPARK PLUGS)

Check wires, rotor, distributor cap, spark plugs, points, timing, and so forth spring and fall, more often under hard use. Replace spark plugs every fall for better cold-weather starting. Replace other parts as needed.

OIL AND FILTER

Change every three to six months, depending on heaviness of use and extremity of climate. Change weight of oil according to season. Aim to change every 3,000 miles.

POWER STEERING

Check fluid at every oil change (three to six months).

TIRES AND WHEEL BALANCE
Rotate spring and fall. Balance every time front wheel worked on.

WHEEL BEARINGS
Repack front bearings every spring.

WINDSHIELD WIPER BLADES
Replace as needed in dry climates, spring and fall where rainy.

Seasonal Maintenance List

EVERY TIME OIL AND FILTER ARE CHANGED (SPRING AND FALL, OR FOUR TIMES A YEAR—DEPENDING ON SEVERITY OF CLIMATE AND USE):

- Check automatic transmission fluid level
- Check air filter
- Check brakes
- Check for leaks
- Check cooling system
- Check crankcase ventilator valve
- Check power steering fluid
- Do chassis lubrication

EVERY TIME THE IGNITION SYSTEM IS CHECKED (SPRING AND FALL):

- Rotate tires and balance wheels
- Have front end aligned
- Check emission system

- Replace fuel filter
- Wax or polish car
- Service air conditioner (for year-around use)
- Change windshield wipers (in rainy, snowy climates)

EVERY SPRING:

- Repack front wheel bearings
- Service air conditioner (for seasonal use)

EVERY FALL:

- Have spark plugs changed
- Have a complete diagnostic

MONTHLY:

- Have battery and accessories checked
- Check for any frayed or worn lines, wires, etc.
- Wash car—more often is even better

WEEKLY:

- Run air conditioner for ten minutes

Appendix B

STATE OFFICES DEALING WITH AUTOMOTIVE CONSUMER AFFAIRS & SUMMARY OF STATE LEMON LAWS

(Under Lemon Law summaries, the first sentence summarizes the state definition of a lemon, while the second instructs the consumer how to proceed.)

ALABAMA
Consumer Protection Division, Office of Attorney General, 138 Adams Avenue, Montgomery, AL 36130, (205) 261-4200

LEMON LAW: NONE

ALASKA
Consumer Protection Section, Dept. of Law, 1031 W. Fourth Avenue, Suite 110, Anchorage, AK 99501, (907) 279-0428

LEMON LAW: 3 unsuccessful repairs or car under repair for 30 business days within first year or warranty period. Write manufacturer and dealer by certified mail explaining the problem and demanding they refund or replace within 60 days.

ARIZONA

Financial Fraud Division, Office of Attorney General, 1275 W. Washington, Room 259, Phoenix, AZ 85007, (602) 279-3702

LEMON LAW: 4 unsuccessful repairs or car under repair for 30 calendar days within shorter of 1 year or warranty. Written notice to manufacturer along with opportunity to repair.

ARKANSAS

Consumer Protection Division, Office of Attorney General, Justice Building, Little Rock, AR 72201, (501) 371-2341

LEMON LAW: NONE

CALIFORNIA

Department of Consumer Affairs, 1020 N Street, Room 516, Sacramento, CA 95814, (916) 445-4465

LEMON LAW: 4 unsuccessful repairs or car under repair for 31 calendar days within shorter of 1 year or 12,000 miles. Inform manufacturer in writing of need for repair. California has a certified procedure for arbitration.

COLORADO

Antitrust & Consumer Protection, Dept. of Law, 1525 Sherman Street, 2nd floor, Denver, CO 80203, (303) 866-3611

LEMON LAW: 4 unsuccessful repairs or car under repair for 30 business days within shorter of 1 year or warranty. Write manufacturer by certified mail and give opportunity to repair.

CONNECTICUT

Commissioner, Consumer Protection Department, 165 Capitol Avenue, Hartford, CT 06106, (203) 566-4999

LEMON LAW: 4 unsuccessful repairs or car under repair for 30 calendar days within shorter of 2 years or 18,000 miles; *or* 2 repairs of a hazardous defect within shorter of 1 year or warranty. Written report to manufacturer, agent or authorized dealer. Connecticut offers an arbitration program.

USED CAR LEMON LAW: contact State Attorney General's Office for details.

DELAWARE

Division of Consumer Affairs, Department of Community Affairs, 820 N. French Street, 4th floor, Wilmington, DE 19801, (302) 571-3250

LEMON LAW: 4 unsuccessful repairs or car under repair for 31 calendar days within shorter of 1 year or warranty. Write manufacturer and give opportunity to repair.

DISTRICT OF COLUMBIA

Office of Consumer Education & Information, 614 H Street, NW, Room 108, Washington, DC 20001, (202) 727-7067

LEMON LAW: 4 unsuccessful repairs or car under repair for 30 calendar days, *or* one unsuccessful repair of hazardous defect, within shorter of 2 years or 18,000 miles. Notify manufacturer, agent, or authorized dealer. D.C. offers an arbitration program.

FLORIDA
Division of Consumer Services, Agriculture & Consumer Services Department, Mayo Bldg., Tallahassee, FL 32301, (904) 487-6900

LEMON LAW: 3 unsuccessful repairs or car under repair for 15 business days within shorter of 1 year or warranty. Notify manufacturer in writing. Florida offers an arbitration program.

GEORGIA
Office of Consumer Affairs, Office of Budget and Planning, 205 Butler Street, SE, Plaza-E, Atlanta, GA 30334, (404) 656-1760

LEMON LAW: NONE

HAWAII
Office of Consumer Protection, 250 South King Street, Room 520, Honolulu, HI 96813, (808) 548-2560

LEMON LAW: 3 unsuccessful repairs or car under repair for 30 business days within warranty. Write manufacturer and give opportunity to repair. Hawaii offers an arbitration program.

IDAHO
Office of Attorney General, Statehouse, Boise, ID 83720, (208) 334-2400

LEMON LAW: NONE

ILLINOIS
Attorney General, 500 S. Spring Street, Springfield, IL 62706, (217) 782-1090

LEMON LAW: 4 unsuccessful repairs or car under repair for 30 business days within shorter of 1 year or 12,000 miles. Write manufacturer and give opportunity to repair.

INDIANA
Division of Consumer Protection, Office of Attorney General, 125 W. Market, Indianapolis, IN 46204, (317) 232-6331

LEMON LAW: 4 unsuccessful repairs or car under repair for 30 business days within shorter of 18 months or 18,000 miles. Write manufacturer to give opportunity to repair, only if written notice is required by warranty.

IOWA
Consumer Protection Division, Office of Attorney General, Hoover State Office Building, Des Moines, IA 50319, (515) 281-5926

LEMON LAW: 4 unsuccessful repairs or car under repair for 30 calendar days within shorter of 1 year or 12,000 miles. Notify manufacturer and give opportunity to repair.

KANSAS
Deputy Attorney General, Consumer Protection Division, Office of Attorney General, Judicial Center, Topeka, KS 40601, (502) 654-7600

LEMON LAW: 4 unsuccessful repairs or car under repair for 30 calendar days (*or* 10 total repairs) within shorter of 1 year or 12,000 miles. Notify manufacturer.

KENTUCKY
Attorney General, State Capitol, Frankfort, KY 40601, (502) 564-7600

LEMON LAW: 4 unsuccessful repairs or car under repair for 30 calendar days within shorter of 1 year or 12,000 miles. Notify manufacturer in writing.

LOUISIANA
Office of the Attorney General, 900 Riverside N, State Capitol, Baton Rouge, LA 70804, (504) 342-7013

LEMON LAW: 4 unsuccessful repairs or car under repair for 30 calendar days within shorter of 1 year or 12,000 miles. Notify manufacturer or authorized dealer.

MAINE
Bureau of Consumer Credit Protection, Dept. of Professional & Financial Regulation, State House Station #35, Augusta, ME 04333, (207) 289-3731

LEMON LAW: 3 unsuccessful repairs or car under repair for 15 business days within shorter of 2 years or 18,000 miles. Notify manufacturer or authorized dealer, in writing if warranty or manual requires. Manufacturer has 7 business days to comply.

MARYLAND
Consumer & Investor Affairs Division, Office of Attorney General, 7 N. Calvery Street, Baltimore, MD 21202, (301) 576-6550

LEMON LAW: 4 unsuccessful repairs or car under repair for 30 days, or 1 unsuccessful repair or failure of either steering or braking system, within shorter of 15 months or 15,000 miles. Write manufacturer by certified mail, return receipt requested, and give opportunity to repair.

MASSACHUSETTS
Executive Office of Consumer Affairs, One Ashburton Place, Boston, MA 02108, (617) 717-7755

LEMON LAW: 3 unsuccessful repairs or car under repair for 15 business days within shorter of 1 year or 15,000 miles. Notify manufacturer or authorized dealer, who have 7 business days to repair. Massachusetts offers an arbitration program.

USED CAR LEMON LAW: contact State Attorney General's Office.

MICHIGAN
Director, Regulatory & Consumer Affairs; PSC—Department of Commerce, P.O. Box 30221, Lansing, MI 48909, (517) 334-6430

LEMON LAW: 4 unsuccessful repairs or car under repair for 30 calendar days within shorter of 1 year or warranty. Notify manufacturer by certified mail, return receipt requested; they have 5 business days to repair.

MINNESOTA
Assistant Attorney General, Consumer Division, Office of Attorney General, 117 University Avenue, 1st Floor, Ford Office Building, St. Paul, MN 55155, (612) 296-775

LEMON LAW: 4 unsuccessful repairs or car under repair for 30 business days, *or* 1 unsuccessful repair of hazardous braking or steering loss, within shorter of 2 years or warranty. Notify manufacturer, agent or authorized dealer in writing, giving opportunity to repair.

USED CAR LEMON LAW: contact State Attorney General's office.

MISSISSIPPI
Director, Consumer Protection Division, Office of Attorney General, Gartin Building, 5th Floor, Jackson, MS 39201, (601) 359-3680

LEMON LAW: 3 unsuccessful repairs or car under repair for 15 business days, within shorter of 1 year or warranty. Notify manufacturer in writing, giving opportunity to repair.

MONTANA
Attorney-Unit Manager, Consumer Affairs Unit, Department of Commerce, 1424 Ninth Avenue, Helena, MT 59620, (406) 444-4313

LEMON LAW: 4 unsuccessful repairs or car under repair for 30 business days, within shorter of 2 years or 18,000 miles. Notify manufacturer in writing, giving opportunity to repair.

NEBRASKA
Consumer Fraud Section, Office of Attorney General, P.O. Box 94906, Lincoln, NE 68509, (402) 471-3833

LEMON LAW: 4 unsuccessful repairs or car under repair for 40 days, within shorter of 1 year or warranty. Notify manufacturer by certified mail, giving opportunity to repair.

NEVADA

Commissioner, Division of Consumer Affairs, Department of Commerce, 2501 E. Sahara Avenue #202, Las Vegas, NV 89518, (702) 386-5293

LEMON LAW: 4 unsuccessful repairs or car under repair for 30 calendar days, within shorter of 1 year or warranty. Notify manufacturer in writing.

NEW HAMPSHIRE

Attorney General, 208 State House Annex, 235 Capitol Street, Concord, NH 03301, (603) 271-3658

LEMON LAW: 4 unsuccessful repairs or car under repair for 30 business days, within shorter of 1 year or warranty. Notify manufacturer, distributor, agent or authorized dealer.

NEW MEXICO

Director, Consumer Protection & Economic Crimes, Office of Attorney General, Bataan Memorial Building, Santa Fe, NM 87503, (505) 827-6060

LEMON LAW: 4 unsuccessful repairs or car under repair for 30 business days, within shorter of 1 year or warranty. Notify manufacturer, giving opportunity to repair.

NEW YORK

Director, Consumer Protection, Twin Towers, One Commerce Plaza, Albany, NY 12210, (518) 474-3514

LEMON LAW: 4 unsuccessful repairs or car under repair for 30 days, within shorter of 2 years or 18,000 miles. Notify manufacturer, agent or authorized dealer. New York also offers an arbitration program.

USED CAR LEMON LAW: contact State Attorney General's office.

NORTH CAROLINA
Deputy Attorney General, Consumer Protection Division, Department of Justice, Justice Bldg., Box 629, Raleigh, NC 27602

LEMON LAW: 4 unsuccessful repairs within shorter of 2 years or 24,000 miles or warranty, *or* car under repair for 20 business days during any 12 month period under warranty. Written notice (if required by warranty or owner's manual) to manufacturer, giving opportunity to repair within 15 calendar days.

NORTH DAKOTA
Attorney, Consumer Fraud Division, Office of Attorney General, 17th Floor, State Capitol, Bismark, ND 58505, (701) 224-3404

LEMON LAW: 4 unsuccessful repairs or car under repair for 30 business days, within shorter of 1 year or warranty. Notify manufacturer, giving opportunity to repair.

OHIO
Consumers Counsel, Office of Consumers Counsel, 137 East Street, Columbus, OH 43266, (614) 466-9545

LEMON LAW: 3 unsuccessful repairs or car under repair for 30 days, *or* 8 total repairs, *or* 1 unsuccessful repair of hazardous defect, within shorter of 1 year or 18,000 miles. Notify manufacturer, agent, or authorized dealer.

OKLAHOMA
Administrator, Consumer Credit Department, 2101 N. Lincoln Blvd., Oklahoma City, OK 73105, (405) 521-3653

LEMON LAW: 4 unsuccessful repairs or car under repair for 45 calendar days, within shorter of 1 year or warranty. Notify manufacturer in writing, giving opportunity to repair.

OREGON
Chief Counsel, Division of Consumer Protection & Services, Department of Justice, 520 S Yamhill, Portland, OR 97204, (503) 229-5548

LEMON LAW: 4 unsuccessful repairs or car under repair for 30 business days, within shorter of 1 year or 12,000 miles. Notify manufacturer in writing, giving opportunity to repair.

PENNSYLVANIA
Director, Bureau of Consumer Protection, Office of Attorney General, Strawberry Square, 14th Floor, Harrisburg, PA 17120, (717) 787-9707

LEMON LAW: 3 unsuccessful repairs or car under repair for 30 calendar days, for problem that first appeared within shortest of warranty, 1 year or 12,000 miles. Deliver to authorized service facility; if not in condition to deliver, written notice to manufacturer or repair facility requires them to arrange and pay for delivery.

RHODE ISLAND
Executive Director, Consumers' Counsel, 365 Broadway, Providence, RI 02902, (401) 277-2764

LEMON LAW: 4 unsuccessful repairs or car under repair for 30 calendar days, within shorter of 1 year or 15,000 miles. Notify manufacturer or authorized dealer, giving 15 days to repair.

USED CAR LEMON LAW: contact State Attorney General's office.

SOUTH CAROLINA

Administrator, Department of Consumer Affairs, 2221 Devine Street, P.O. Box 5757, Columbia, SC 29250, (803) 734-9458

LEMON LAW: NONE

SOUTH DAKOTA

Assistant Attorney General, Division of Consumer Affairs, Office of Attorney General, State Capitol, Pierre, SD 57501, (605) 773-4400

LEMON LAW: NONE

TENNESSEE

Director, Division of Consumer Affairs, Department of Commerce & Insurance, 206 State Office Building, Nashville, TN 37219, (615) 741-4737

LEMON LAW: 4 unsuccessful repairs or car under repair for 30 business days, within shorter of 1 year or warranty. Notify manufacturer by certified mail.

TEXAS

Director, Division of Consumer Affairs, Office of Attorney General, P.O. Box 12548, Austin, TX 78711, (512) 463-2097

LEMON LAW: 4 unsuccessful repairs or car under repair for 30 days, within shorter of 1 year or warranty. Written notice to manufacturer, giving opportunity to repair.

UTAH
Consumer Services, Department of Business Regulation, 160 E. 300 Street, Salt Lake City, UT 84110, (801) 530-6645

LEMON LAW: 4 unsuccessful repairs or car under repair for 30 business days, within shorter of 1 year or warranty. Report to manufacturer, agent or authorized dealer.

VERMONT
Chief of Public Protection Division, Office of Attorney General, 109 State Street, Montpelier, VT 05602, (802) 828-3171

LEMON LAW: 3 unsuccessful repairs or car under repair for 30 calendar days, within warranty. Report to manufacturer, granting 30 days to repair. State provides arbitration procedure.

VIRGINIA
Director, Consumer Affairs Office, Agriculture & Consumer Services Department, 1100 Bank Street, Richmond, VA 23219, (804) 786-2042

LEMON LAW: 4 unsuccessful repairs or car under repair for 30 calendar days within 1 year. Report to manufacturer in writing, granting 15 days for last attempt to repair.

WASHINGTON
Office of Consumer Protection, Office of Attorney General, Dexter Horton Building, Seattle, WA 98104, (206) 464-6254

LEMON LAW: 4 unsuccessful repairs or car under repair for 30 calendar days, *or* two repairs for hazardous defects, first reported within shortest of warranty, 24 months, or 24,000 miles. Report to manufacturer in writing.

WEST VIRGINIA
Deputy Attorney General, Consumer Protection Division, Office of Attorney General, 1204 Kanawha Blvd., East Charleston, WV 25305, (304) 348-8986

LEMON LAW: 3 unsuccessful repairs or car under repair for 30 calendar days, within shorter of 1 year or warranty, *or* 1 unsuccessful repair of highly hazardous defect. Report in writing to manufacturer, granting opportunity to repair.

WISCONSIN
Unit Head, Consumer Protection & Antitrust Unit, Department of Justice, P.O. Box 7856, Madison, WI 53707, (608) 266-2426

LEMON LAW: 4 unsuccessful repairs or car under repair for 30 days, within shorter of 1 year or warranty. Report to manufacturer or any authorized dealer.

WYOMING
Assistant Attorney General, Office of Attorney General, State Capitol, Cheyenne, WY 82002, (307) 777-7841

LEMON LAW: 4 unsuccessful repairs or car under repair for 30 business days, within 1 year. Report to manufacturer in writing, granting opportunity to repair.

CANADA
Consumers' Association of Canada, P.O. Box 9300, Ottawa, Ont. K1G 3T9, (613) 723-0187

Canadians are also recommended to contact the Executive Council of the Solicitor General's office of their respective provinces.

OTHER HELPFUL GROUPS AND AGENCIES

AID FOR LEMON OWNERS
21711 West Ten Mile Road, Suite 210
Southfield, MI 48075
(313) 354-1760

AMERICAN LEMON CLUB
205 East Southern Avenue
Covington, KY 41015
(606) 431-5393

CENTER FOR AUTO SAFETY
2001 S Street, NW, Suite 410
Washington, DC 20009

NATIONAL HIGHWAY TRAFFIC SAFETY ADMINISTRATION TOLL-FREE DAY-AND-NIGHT HOTLINE
1-800-424-9393
1-800-424-9153 (for hearing impaired)
This organization will refer you to appropriate federal, state, and local authorities.

Glossary

*Bold-faced words or phrases within a
definition refer to the chapter that establishes
a context for the defined term*

ACCELERATOR—technical term for "gas pedal." Actually controls flow of fuel-air mix from **carburetor** to engine.

ADDITIVE—any chemical added to fuel or other fluids to improve effectiveness or clean or seal some part.

ADVANCE TIMING (OR SPARK)—to reset **ignition** so that sparking occurs sooner.

AIR FILTER (OR CLEANER)—a device to clean air before it enters the **carburetor** or fuel-injection system. Any device to separate out the dirt from air.

AIR-FUEL RATIO—the proportion of air to gasoline mixed by the **carburetor** or fuel-injection system for use as fuel in the **internal combustion** system.

AIR SPRING—a system for using air instead of metal springs, used in the **suspension** system of some innovative cars.

ALIGNMENT—positioning the various parts in a system so that they function correctly—as in "wheel alignment," which affects **steering** and **suspension.**

ALTERNATOR—a device for **generating** electric current.

ANTIFREEZE—a chemical added to water to prevent winter freezing and summer overheating of the **cooling** system.

ANTIKNOCK—substances added to gasoline to improve performance and stop knocking, pinging noises in the **engine.**

AUTOMATIC TRANSMISSION—a system in which energy is transferred from the engine to the wheels by **transmission** gears that adjust themselves automatically, without the driver having to make the choice.

AXLE—a shaft that holds on, drives, and/or supports revolving wheels as part of the **suspension** system.

BACKFIRE—explosion of unburned fuel mixture in the **exhaust** system, usually due to faulty spark plugs.

BALANCE (TIRE)—the addition of small weights to a wheel to make up for imperfections in the tire. An aspect of **suspension.**

BALL JOINT—ball-and-socket type of flexible joint, used in steering and **suspension** systems.

BATTERY CAPACITY—amount of current a battery is capable of receiving, **generating,** and storing.

BATTERY CHARGING—the renewal of a battery's electrical **generating** capacity.

BATTERY (MAINTENANCE-FREE)—a battery sealed so as to need no additional electrolyte. **Generating.**

BATTERY TERMINALS—protruding posts on battery, to which cables are attached. **Starting, generating.**

BATTERY TEST—a means of measuring the battery's state of charge. **Generating.**

BEARING—a device that guides, positions, and reduces friction between fixed and moving parts. Used in many systems.

BELTED BIAS—a kind of tire with crisscrossed plies and "belts" beneath the treads. **Suspension.**

BELTS—V-shaped belts using pulleys to transfer power from the crankshaft to the fan, the power-steering pump, etc. Used in many systems.

BENDIX GEAR—a gear that engages automatically with the flywheel when the **starter** turns on, then disengages automatically when the engine starts.

BIAS PLY—a kind of tire with crisscrossed plies but no "belts" beneath the treads. **Suspension.**

BLEEDING—removing any fluid, air, etc. from any system.

BLEEDING THE BRAKES—removal of air from hydrolic **braking** system.

BLOCK—lower portion of the **engine** that contains the cylinders, pistons, piston rings, connecting rods, crankshaft, etc.

BOILING POINT—temperature at which a liquid boils and becomes a gas—differing from one liquid to another. **Cooling system.**

BRAKE, DISC—a system using calipers to force a wheel to stop. Highly resistent to wetness, fade, etc. Usually used for front-wheel **braking.**

BRAKE, DRUM—a system in which "shoes" are rubbed against a metal drum to stop a wheel. Usually used for rear-wheel **braking;** doubles as parking brake.

BRAKE LINE—tube that carries brake fluid from master cylinder to wheels. **Braking.**

BRAKE LINING—friction-producing material attached to brake shoes in drum **braking** system.

BRAKE SHOES—in drum **braking** system, the lined part that is forced against the drum to stop the car.

BREAKER POINTS—points of contact within the distributor that open and close **ignition** circuits.

CALIPER—in disc **braking,** the part that produces clamping action.

CAM—an eccentric (off-center) wheel on a shaft, which is used to produce up-and-down motion on an engaged part. *See* **camshaft.**

CAMSHAFT—a shaft with cams that operates the valves in the **engine.**

CARBON—byproduct of internal combustion, which can remain as deposits on **engine** parts.

CARBURETOR—system used to mix fuel and air.

CATALYTIC CONVERTER—chemical-pollution control device for the **exhaust** system.

CHARGE (BATTERY)—restoration of the battery's charge by passing electric current into it. **Generating.**

CHASSIS—Frame and working parts, aside from body and fenders, related to **suspension.**

CHOKE—valve in **carburetor** works automatically to enrich air-fuel mix for cold starts.

CLEARANCE—amount of space between two working parts.

CLUTCH—used in cars having a standard **transmission,** the coupling device that connects and disconnects the engine.

COIL—in **ignition** system, device to increase battery voltage to high voltage, in order to activate spark plugs.

COMBUSTION—burning, such as occurs in the **engine.**

COMBUTION CHAMBER—in **internal combustion,** the area formed by piston, cylinder, and head, in which combustion takes place. Also called the "compression chamber."

COMPRESSION—applying pressure to anything to reduce its volume, as in the compression chambers of the **engine.**

COMPRESSION CHAMBER—same as "combustion chamber."

COMPRESSION CHECK OR TEST—a test of the cylinders' compression to diagnose the condition of the **engine** valves and/or rings.

COMPRESSION GAUGE—device used to register compression in a compression test of the **engine.**

CONDENSER—in **air conditioning,** a component that cools heated gaseous Freon and turns it back into a liquid.

CONDENSER—in **ignition** system, a device that absorbs surges of electricity.

CONNECTING ROD—in the **engine,** the link between a piston and the crankshaft.

CONTACT BREAKER POINTS—in **ignition,** the contacts where the primary circuit to the coil is made and broken, to induce the high-tension sparks that are distributed to the spark plugs.

COOLANT—any fluid used in **cooling** system.

CRANKSHAFT—bent shaft that runs the length of **engine,** to which the connecting rods are attached.

CV (CONSTANT VELOCITY) JOINTS—in front wheel drive suspension systems, the joints that allow for changes in driving angles and direction.

CYLINDER—in the **engine,** the bores (holes) in which the pistons move up and down.

CYLINDER HEAD—same as "head." Top section of the **engine,** containing the valves, bolted on top of the block to form the combustion chambers. The relative size and power of engines depends on the number of cylinders, usually four, six, or eight.

DETERGENT—chemical additive for gasoline, oil, etc., to clean out deposits or unclog **engine** or other parts.

DETONATION—the too-rapid burning of the fuel-and-air mixture, apparent during acceleration as a rapid metalic **engine** noise, caused by low-grade fuel or **ignition** timing being too far advanced. Also called "knocking" or "pinging."

DIAGNOSIS—analysis of symptoms to arrive at causes.

DIESEL ENGINE—internal combustion system using diesel oil instead of gasoline, **fuel injection** instead of carburetion, and highly compressed air to ignite the fuel.

DIESELING—Continued running of engine and burning of fuel after car is turned off. Also called "running on." Discussed under **carburetor.**

DIFFERENTIAL—in **suspension** system, part that drives rear axles and allows for different wheel speeds during turns.

DIMMER SWITCH—in **electrical** system, switch that changes headlight beams from high to low.

DIPSTICK—in **lubricating** system, rod used to measure how much oil is in the oil pan.

DISC BRAKES—system of **braking** in which padded calipers pinch a rotating disc to effect braking.

DISTRIBUTOR—device that distributes the spark to the spark plug cables for **ignition.**

DISTRIBUTOR CAP—the cover over the distributor, into which fit the incoming coil wire and outgoing spark plug cables of the **ignition** system.

DOWNSHIFT—shifting to a "lower" **transmission** gear, as from third to second.

DRIVE TRAIN—the components through which the power generated in the combustion chambers is transmitted to the wheels. Also called **power train.**

ELECTROLYTE—in **generating** system, acid-and-water mix in battery.

ELECTRONIC—using transistors, computers, in high-tech systems.

EMERGENCY BRAKE—*See* **parking brake.**

EMISSIONS—polluting byproducts of burning fuel released through the **exhaust** system.

ENGINE—such as the "internal combustion" **engine,** any device that makes use of heat energy to create useful motion.

EXHAUST MANIFOLD—pipe connecting **exhaust** ports with exhaust pipe, which in turn connects with the muffler.

EXHAUST VALVE—valve that feeds exhaust gases from **engine** system into exhaust manifold.

FAIR PRICE FORMULA—a system for estimating repair costs by calculating and adding together realistic prices for labor and parts.

FLOAT—part of **carburetor** that floats on the fuel, working with "needle valve" to control fuel level.

FLOODING—condition in which too much or too-rich fuel has reached the **carburetor** system, preventing the car from starting.

FLUSH—to clean out by a quick flow of water or other fluid.

FLYWHEEL—wheel, attached to crankshaft, that stores energy essential for momentum of **engine** and **transmission.**

FOUR-STROKE CYCLE—in the **engine,** the process each piston goes through each time it fires.

FOUR-WHEEL DRIVE—a system that allows all four wheels to be used to drive a car, for better traction and safety.

FRAME—in **suspension** system, the part that supports the car body and to which parts are attached.

FREON—the refrigerant used in **air conditioning.**

FRICTION—heat-producing wear, occurring when moving parts are in contact.

FRONT-WHEEL DRIVE—a system in which a car is "pulled" by the front wheels instead of being "pushed" by the rear wheels.

FUSE—protective device that breaks the flow of excessive **electrical** current.

GASKET—compressible, lightweight material placed between metal parts as a seal.

GEAR—a toothed wheel or other machine part that meshes with a similarly toothed part, so that one drives the other.

GLOW PLUG—part of the diesel system, heated by electricity to ignite fuel from a cold start.

GOING RATE—the customary, average, or standard price (for labor) in a particular locality.

GROUND (BATTERY)—connecting of negative terminal to framework of car. Described under **generating** system.

HAND BRAKE—*See* **parking brake.**

HOT SPOT—an area much hotter than surrounding areas, often caused in the **engine** by carbon deposits.

HYDRAULIC—controlled or powered by fluid in motion.

IDLING—engine turning over slowly, but not transmitting power, as when in neutral **transmission** gear.

IGNITION SWITCH—driver-operated by key to turn on **ignition** and **electrical** systems.

INDEPENDENT SUSPENSION—system that allows each wheel to work independently.

INJECTOR—pump that squirts measured amount of fuel into the combustion chambers of the **engine.**

INTAKE MANIFOLD—tubes connecting **carburetor** to the head of the **engine.**

INTAKE VALVE—**engine** valve that allows fuel-air mixture into a combustion chamber.

INTERNAL COMBUSTION SYSTEM—a system in which the force of contained explosions under pressure is used to provide power. In the car, this is equivalent to the **engine.**

KNOCKING—noise caused by detonation (part of fuel mix burning too fast) in the **engine.**

LEADED GAS—gas containing lead-based chemicals that prevent knocking but that cause polluting **exhaust** and also damage or destroy catalytic converters.

LEAN MIXTURE—air-and-fuel mix formed in **carburetor** with less fuel and more air than normal.

LONG BLOCK—The complete **engine,** including both head and block.

LUBRICANT—material such as oil, used in **lubrication** system to reduce friction between working parts.

MACPHERSON STRUT—alternative **suspension** system built-in device, unifying functions of spring with shock absorber.

MAIN BEARINGS—in the **engine,** the crankshaft supports.

MANIFOLD—a set of pipes that connects a set of holes to a single common hole. See **Intake manifold.**

MASTER CYLINDER—in the **brake** system, the unit that provides hydraulic pressure.

MISFIRING—the failure of one or more **engine** cylinders to fire in normal order.

MISSING—when one of more **engine** cylinders fails to operate.

MUFFLER—device for treating **exhaust** gases, to reduce engine noise.

MULTI-VISCOSITY OILS—combination of light- and heavy-weight oils (such as SAE 10W–30 or 10W–40) for use in the **lubrication** system under a wide variety of temperatures and conditions.

NOZZLE—hole through which fuel is squirted, specifically in **carburetor** and **fuel-injection** systems.

OCTANE RATING—the measure of the antiknock or antidetonation properties of **engine** gasoline. The higher the rating, the more antiknock elements present.

OIL CLASSIFICATION—grading of **lubricating** oil for use in various types of vehicles and engines.

OVERHAUL (MAJOR)—ideally, to bring an **engine** (or other system) into the equivalent of a new condition by a combination of renewing, replacing, and/or repairing of parts.

OVERHAUL (MINOR)—to bring a part of a system into like-new condition by replacement and/or repairing of some parts.

OVERHEATING—the inability of the **cooling system** to maintain normal engine-running temperature.

PARKING BRAKE—also called "handbrake," although sometimes operated by foot. Locks rear wheels, or sometimes the transmission.

PINGING—rattling noise in the **engine** during acceleration, usually caused by poor fuel or too-advanced ignition timing.

PISTON—in **engine,** a plunger that slides up and down in a cylinder.

PISTON RINGS—in **engine,** the rings set in the sides of the piston to seal the combustion chamber, above, from the rest of the system, below.

PLUG GAPPING—in the **ignition** system, the proper adjustment of the spark plug electrodes relative to one another.

PLY—the rubberized fabric strip of which tires are made.

POINTS—in the **ignition** system, the points of electrical contact in contact breaker.

POSITIVE TERMINAL—in the **generating** system, the terminal marked "+" on the battery.

POWER STEERING—system to reduce driver's effort in **steering** by means of a hydraulic boost.

POWER TRAIN—same as **drive train.**

PREIGNITION—condition in which the air-fuel mixture in the **engine** cylinders is ignited too soon.

PROPORTIONING VALVE—in **braking,** a device for coordinating front and rear brakes, so that they stop together.

RACK AND PINION GEARBOX—a **steering** mechanism on higher-priced small cars.

RADIAL TIRE—a comparatively costly, long-life tire in which the plies are at right angles to the tread, which is reinforced by belts. Discussed under **suspension.**

REAR-WHEEL DRIVE—traditional system in which the car is "pushed" or "driven" by the rear wheels.

RESISTOR—in **ignition** systems, a device to lower voltage and flow of current to the coil.

RESONATOR—minimuffler in tail pipe, to further reduce noise of **exhaust.**

RETARD TIMING—in the **ignition** system, to set back the timing of the sparks. The opposite of "advance timing."

RICH MIXTURE—in **carburetors** or **fuel injectors,** a higher ratio of fuel to air than normal. The opposite of "lean mixture."

RIDING THE CLUTCH—bad habit of keeping a foot on the standard **transmission** clutch pedal while driving the car.

RING JOB—a major **engine** repair, entailing the replacement of rings and reconditioning of cylinders.

ROCKER ARM—part of **engine** controlling push rods and valve stems.

"RUNNING ON"—*See* **dieseling.**

SHIFT FORKS—used in standard **transmission** to move the gears.

SHIFT RAILS—sliding rods used in standard **transmission,** to carry the "shift forks" to the gears.

SHIMMY —the side-to-side shaking of the front wheels, due to poor **suspension.**

SHOCK ABSORBER—means of minimizing spring bounce in **suspension.**

SHORT BLOCK—the **engine** block only, exclusive of the head.

SHORT CIRCUIT—interruption of an **electrical** current before it reaches its destination.

SIDEWALL—side portion of a tire, which carries the size and other information. Discussed under **suspension.**

SOLENOID—in the **starter** system, an electric switch that connects the battery to the starter motor.

SPARK—in **ignition** system, a current of electricity that jumps the gap in a spark plug.

SPARK GAP—the gap between the electrodes on a spark plug.

SPARK PLUG—in the **ignition** system, removable plug, housing the electrodes and spark gap and to which distributor cables are attached.

SPRING—in the **suspension** system, any device that will return to its original shape after being compressed or stretched and can be used for cushioning the ride.

STALL—to stop functioning while in operation—usually caused by **carburetor** malfunction.

STARTER MOTOR—in the **starter** system, an electric motor that drives a gear that turns the engine over.

STICK SHIFT—standard manual **transmission** system.

TAIL PIPE—last section of exhaust system.

TAPPET—in the **engine,** a screw that adjusts clearances in the valve system.

TAPPET NOISE—engine clatter caused by too much valve clearance.

THERMOSTAT—in the **cooling** system, a sensor that controls rate of flow of coolant to the engine.

THROTTLE—a valve in the **carburetor** controlled by the foot pedal that meters out the fuel-and-air mixture going to the cylinders.

TIMING—coordination of events in different systems; in the **engine,** to activate the ignition spark and valves in relation to the crankshaft.

TIRE BALANCE—the addition of weights to the wheels, to insure the tires turn and wear smoothly. **Suspension.**

TIRE ROTATION—switching tires from front to rear and side to side to insure evenness of wear. **Suspension.**

TIRE TREAD—the flat portion of the tire that rolls on the road.

TOE-IN AND TOE-OUT—aspects of wheel alignment. **Suspension.**

TORQUE—force used to create rotation in the **engine.** Also, a measurement of engine power.

TORSION BAR SUSPENSION—a **suspension** system used in some cars to replace springs with a bar that provides springing action.

TRACTION—friction between tires and road, necessary for both driving and stopping, but also wearing to tires.

TRANSFORMER OR COIL—part of **generating** system, used to boost voltage.

TRANSMISSION—several variant systems using gears to adjust the rate that power is sent from the engine to the wheels, to accord with variations in speed, road conditions, load, etc.

TUNE-UP—maintenance procedure to check, adjust, repair, and time **ignition** and related systems, to bring them into the best possible coordinated working order.

TURBOCHARGER—in the **carburetor,** a system that increases power and fuel economy by forcing extra air into the combustion chambers.

UNIVERSAL JOINTS—in the **suspension** system, flexible joints that allow for changes in driving angle and direction.

UNLEADED GASOLINE—fuel free of tetraethyl lead. Required by cars with catalytic converters. Affects both **engine** and **exhaust.**

UPSHIFT—in **transmission,** the shifting into a "higher" gear—i.e., from second to third.

VALVE—in the **engine** and elsewhere, a unit that opens and closes a hole.

VALVE GRINDING—in **engine** repair, grinding down valve faces to renew and provide tight fit.

VAPOR LOCK—in the **fuel** system, the boiling over and vaporizing of fuel due to failure in cooling. Causes stalling.

VOLTAGE REGULATOR—device to regulate voltage and current in the **generating** system.

WATER PUMP—Cooling system pump.

WHEEL ALIGNMENT—adjustment of wheel angles to assure smoothest driving and least wear to the tires and **suspension** system.

WHEEL BALANCING—adjustment of wheels by adding small lead weights to reduce wear to tires and **suspension.**

WHEEL CYLINDER—the part of the hydraulic **brake** system that applies pressure from the master cylinder to the brake shoes.

Index

To make this index easier for you to use:

1) You will be directed only to passages that directly pertain to the listed entries.

2) Aspects and components of particular systems will be listed, wherever practical, under those systems.

3) Because the names of popular automobile makes, the *Chilton Guide*, the *Fair Price Formula*, and such terms as *mechanic* are referred to so frequently, merely casual references have not been listed.

4) Page numbers in italics refer to illustrations.